A
Plain Brown Rapper

by
Rita Mae Brown

Illustrated by
Sue Sellars

Diana Press

Oakland, California

Acknowledgements

Each of the following people contributed to my being able to put this book together, although the essays do not reflect their political opinions, only my own. Without them my move to Boston would have been an unqualified disaster.

Philip Castle, Sylvia Kaneko, Linda Lecoq, John Lecoq, Pat Mitchell, Nan Poor, Marilyn Salenger, Elaine Spaulding, Byrd Swift, Sarah Wenig, Diana Williamson

A
Plain Brown Rapper
by
Rita Mae Brown

Illustrated by
Sue Sellars

Library of Congress Cataloging in Publication Data

Brown, Rita Mae.
   A plain brown rapper.

   1. Lesbianism —United States—Addresses, essays, lectures. 2. Feminism—United States—Addresses, essays, Lectures. I. Title.
HQ75.6.U5B66   301.41'57'0974   76-50589
ISBN 0-88447-011-3

Dedicated to the Furies Collective

Voting Members
Ginny Berson
Joan Biren
Charlotte Bunch
Tasha Petersen
Sharon Deevey
Helaine Harris
Susan Hathaway
Nancy Myron
Coletta Reid
Lee Schwing
Jennifer Woodul

Non Voting Members
Kara
Cassidy
Michelle
Charly
Frip
Baby Jesus

Contents

Photograph by Nicole Symons

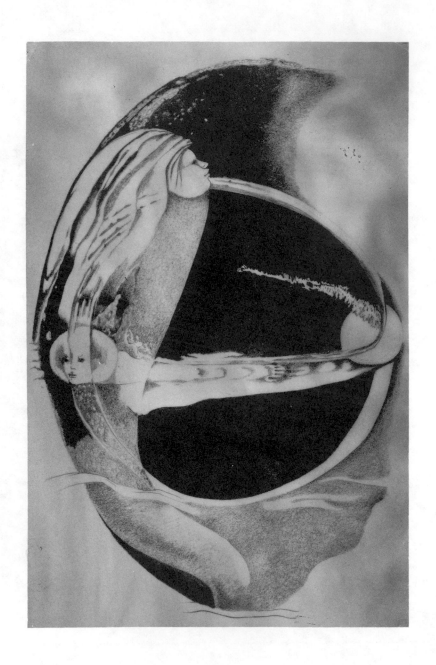

Introduction

Off the coast of Greece in the sixth century before Christ, feminism began as a response to patriarchy. Sappho, a revolutionary despite her wealth (or perhaps because of it), founded her school for women. We are all daughters of those distant mothers. The shrouds of centuries obscure our view. We know little of the school, nothing of its structure. We possess no portrait of its founder.

Through the upheavals, organized brutality, and stunning ignorance which has characterized male supremacy from 600 B.C. until today, there were always a few women and even fewer men, scattered across the globe, who kept the flame of female independence alive. Their names are lost but not their spirit. Their work, their very existence upon this earth makes our work possible. In the mid-1960's we, the inheritors, once again grasped the torch and set the land afire.

The fire passed to me in 1965. Up until that time I'd been rebellious and high spirited. Politics interested me, but then it's fair to say everything interested me. I had no desire to lap a track carrying the torch of revolution over my head. Even though I came from a poor background I was certain my artistic talent would see me through. I would

We are the bridge generation between the desert and the promised land.

become rich and famous, in the order of their importance, take care of my mother, bankroll my friends and gather the lights about me as did Gertrude in Paris in the 1920's.

New York City is America's Paris. I landed there on my feet but broke in the summer of 1965. I was not in the city long, living in an abandoned car with Baby Jesus, a kitten. (She turned eleven on 14 July 1976.) One day B.J. and I walked over to St. Mark's Church in the East Village. I hadn't eaten in a few days and was lonesomer than God. There right in front of me looking quite well-fed was Candice Bergen. B.J. and I had blundered into the filming of "The Group." Candice is one year younger than I so I didn't feel distant from her as I might have from Greta Garbo. Desperately, I wanted to ask her for money for food. I felt sure she'd spring a dollar on my behalf. No matter how hungry I was I couldn't bring myself to beg. So I stood there feeling sicker and sicker as I watched my contemporary recede from me. For the first time in my life it occurred to me that I might remain poor all of my days, that people my own age and also of talent might be forever unreachable because I was too poor to get near them. Sickness transformed into rage. I wanted to go over and yank Candice out of that car she was parked in and yell, "Goddammit, I'm as good as you are. I'm not just a poor asswipe in dirty clothes. I'm an artist! I'm an important person! I'm hungry!" Instead I wandered back to University and Waverly Place because I felt dizzy and weak. The next morning I felt worse. A pizza joint on the other side of Washington Square Park threw its scraps in a garbage can placed on the sidewalk. I had noticed this a few days earlier. I managed to walk over there with B.J. I reached down in the can and picked out a pizza rind and

My St. Mark's revelation drove deeper than fears for my future. I knew there must be millions of people like me all over the world, young, intelligent, with a great deal to offer the societies they lived in yet who by circumstance of birth, race, sex, sex preference were unable to fully develop themselves and were unable to make friendships with those people, just like themselves, who had been born "higher." I always displayed democratic tendoncies but at St. Mark's Church a revolutionary was born.

Revolutionary fervor bubbled throughout New York University in the middle sixties. Thanks to a tuition scholarship I could attend classes as well as meetings dominated by white students in beards. They bored me to tears. Surely revolution was more than hot air? I walked in peace marches and civil rights marches and thought them foolish. Why walk on the road? Why not just walk briskly into General Motors and rip hell out of the joint? If you're going to get hit over the head you might as well get hit for something real as opposed to something symbolic. I quickly understood that the white kids in the civil rights movement and the protest against Viet Nam came from one class while I came from another. Their idea of social change was at variance with my own. They were obsessed with the media which I thought way off the mark. The new Left had a national movement on the tube but no grass roots movement back home.

Giving those people any energy seemed fruitless so I marched less and concentrated more on classes with Conner Cruise O'Brien. I spent a solid year on the debate between Thomas Paine and Edmund Burke. The ideas that enraptured my generation weren't new at all. I was overwhelmed by this discovery and raced to the classics department where I devoured the writings of Sappho, Euripides, Aristophanes, anything I could lay my hands on. Every day I hit on some fantastic idea fully 2000 years old and I recall even now the marvel I experienced at the continuity of human life. These dead souls, in another language, still spoke to me as clearly as if they were in the room and surely they made more sense than the movement heavy in his workshirt. For all my material poverty, those years at New York University bore great riches. I was grounded in the cycles of Western thought. I acquired a solid education. After learning from books I graduated ready to learn from people.

Nineteen sixty-seven, the year before graduation, Martha Shelley, Stephen Donaldson, and I (and others whose names I've unfortunately forgotten) founded Student Homophile League at Columbia and at New York University. The fur flew. "Organized queers!" the administration gasped. "Capitalist decadents!" screamed the New Left. "Diseased whites!" bellowed the Black movement. By declaring our existence we managed to offend all of them. That was enough for me. I knew we were on the right track.

Political activity consumed days, months, years. I charged into the brand new feminist movement in 1968 and the straight women did their best to see I'd charge right back out again. A few diehards are still trying to purge lesbians but we are here to stay. Since then, many women have come out. The difference between feminists who became lesbians and lesbians who became feminists is that the former take great pleasure in principle while the latter make a principle of pleasure. Those women who do choose lesbianism whether by principle or pleasure are at least making that choice themselves rather than bending to relentless heterosexual propaganda.

By now, thanks to those early anti-lesbian campaigns, we've all learned to mistrust a mystique of unity which comes at the expense and silence of minority women. Women who aren't safely white aren't going to be quiet about it, nor are poor women, nor are lesbians. Lesbianism was the first issue to break ideological ground on the real meaning of multiplicity rather than conformity. Because of that initial, bitter struggle I hope the issues of class and white bias can be handled with more maturity than any of us handled the lesbian issue.

In those days I ate, breathed and slept feminism. Nothing else mattered to me. We would bring about a revolution in this nation and we would do it now. My vision of that revolution remains unchanged. However, the timetable undergoes constant revision. Change, it becomes apparent, is not a convulsion of history but the slow, steady push of people over decades.

Such burning intensity culminated in the Furies Collective. I moved to Washington D.C. in 1970 and with the women to whom this book is dedicated organized the Furies Collective. Though none of us were spawned in The Left's nurseries of orthodoxy we operated on a Bolshevik cell model. We lived together, shared chores equally. All clothing rested in a common room. We slept together in mattresses on the floor in the same room. We had desks together if we wanted desks.

This possibility veered towards elitist individualism and Charlotte Bunch and I were forever suspect because we spent so much time at our desks. The only time you could be left alone was in the middle of the night. Consequently, Charlotte and I developed into night people out of self-defense.

We rotated jobs in the outside world except for the two of us that had decent jobs. Work for money was part time so more time could be put into Furies' projects. We created a newspaper which bore our name, a child care center, a school that taught car repair, home repair and self defense. We also wrecked havoc in the community. Our clarity of purpose frightened others. Our self-righteousness exacerbated the paranoia. Within the collective we slaved at study groups. Each woman elected a major country and a minor country. We were to report the history of that nation, the status of women, the economy and current affairs. My major country was the Soviet Union, minor Germany. I felt each in a distinct way had much in common with the U.S.A. Among us we blanketed the earth. Oddly, it didn't occur to us to study the United States until the beginning of our second year together. Precious little time was left for us to enjoy ourselves.

For all our fevers and mistakes, we learned. How we learned. We learned that cadre organizing will never work in the United States. It smacks of conspiracy to people. We learned that you can possess an accurate analysis of the political situation but that doesn't insure people will listen to it especially if you threaten them to begin with. We learned (although the other two poor kids among us already knew this) that a moral appeal will not motivate people as quickly as an appeal to gain--the gain need not be material but that mightily helps. We learned that foreign policy doesn't interest most

Americans as much as domestic policy. We learned that not all women are sisters and not all men are enemies. That one was difficult. We also learned some devastating things about ourselves.

We were all white. A few of us came from lower class backgrounds. The majority were middle class. We ranged in age from 18 to 30 but eight of us were between 22 and 26. Two children were 1½ years old. One girl was 4 years old. We had social direction but few of us had personal direction. In 1971 only Charlotte and I displayed a clear sense of calling. This was to be our undoing. The other women, in time, developed career identities for themselves.

We were all lesbians at that time. As far as I know everyone still is except for two people. We shared a common feminist-socialist philosophy. We thought we knocked down all the walls. What we discovered, painfully, were the real walls that prevent effective political commitments between people.

The first and thickest barrier was that we lied to ourselves about ourselves. Individuals would not admit they were drifting or that their sense of personal identity was threatened primarily by me (devoid of all diplomacy) and secondarily by Charlotte (a diplomat but too talented to trust totally). The stronger the woman was perceived to be the greater the subterranean threat. Charlotte and I were perceived to "run" the collective yet neither Charlotte nor I felt we had any control over the group. By not defining leadership or process we made things far worse than if we'd put down rules.

Our second failing was in refusing to recognize that style is as important as content, politically and individually.

Our third failing was our dismal attempt to

rectify class difference by external means only. We developed a graduated income tax according to one's past privilege and current economic status. As far as that goes it's just and effective. But we ignored the psychology of class differences. In the end, it was this issue and the issue of identity which destroyed our collective.

Women from middle class backgrounds controlled the collective's finances although, again, the rules were unclear. Unspoken assumptions about spending weighed upon us. We poor kids were much more likely to spend our pennies entertaining ourselves than our middle class sisters who needed to feel the money was being put to "good use".

The emotional directness of the poor women, particularly our anger, upset the middle class women. They came from places where communication was indirect, implied. This creates people who search for hidden meanings in your manner, who try to "read" you and then do what they think will gain your approval. Anger was perceived to be on a par with a physical threat, a shocking challenge to integrity. To us, anger was honest communication. You flared up, cooled off and that was the end of it.

Those two examples can give you some idea of the many stylistic differences we encountered. Since these differences were new to each of us, we'd never been in this situation before, we were often frustrated with one another and ourselves. We explored new territory and didn't have a language to describe it. We fell back on the language of the political Left to try and explain the dynamics within the group. As you know, this language is intellectual and corrupted. i.e., Oppression as a term was tossed about so loosely in the early seventies that it became devalued, useless. By the simple act of speaking in this cheapened jargon we lessened our chances to communicate and drew further apart. In this atmosphere a purge loomed inevitable. Joan Biren and Sharon Deevey were unceremoniously tossed out. Straining under the mounting tension, the two women had become moody, petty, bewildered because they felt they were missing or misreading "cues." They acted perfectly human. This was not allowed--*especially* by me.

The Furies began to create within ourselves the dynamic of a fascist state (or Stalinist, take your pick). Like many fascist states we started out on the road to a better life only to be sidetracked by personal weakness. We kept the language of the revolution but the procedure of the Inquisition. There is a difference between fascism as a political system and fascism as personal substance. I was learning this first hand plus I was forewarned because of my study selections, Russia and Germany. In this case forewarned was not forearmed.

We weren't emotionally open with one another and I take the blame for much of that. Sadness, depression, simple complaining disgusted me. I thought those emotions middle class self-indulgence. Given the physical survival battles of my early life, had I allowed myself to experience those emotions I probably would have caved in. At that time I couldn't understand the pattern of middle class women's lives. If you have food on the table, a roof over your head and clothes on your back, what's the problem? The lethal ambivalence with which middle class women live their lives was unknown to me. The only suffering I understood was physical. These women suffered emotionally. I could not fathom this. The malicious seeds of self-doubt were planted in their cribs. They sought their legitimation from others. Their revolution will be when they go cold turkey on their approval addiction and validate their own selves. Political revolution will be when we validate each other and get on with the job of winning political/economic power.

The Furies also did not reckon with the land mines of woman hatred. By becoming a feminist or a lesbian one does not automatically love women. Years of conditioning aren't wiped out so easily. I hated women, somewhat, perhaps less than most of The Furies and more than a very few. Under patriarchy a strong woman is a contradiction in terms. We were not immune from that concept. Since my gifts were more obvious at that time because of the circumstances of my life, I became dangerous. That I had gifts was sin enough. That I refused to apologize for them was unforgivable. That I blatantly enjoyed them was horrendous. The Furies purged me on March 6, 1972.

Charlotte stayed on to try and mend the fences. The Furies folded less than a month later and in the end Charlotte found herself the target.

Tasha Petersen accompanied me on my exile to 217 12th St. S.E. That was the first time in my life I was conscious of anyone standing by me. It may have happened at other times in my life and I couldn't see it. But Tasha, in the midst of our collective collapse, gave me faith. Maybe we were going at this ass-backwards--the personal bonds need to precede the obviously political.

Four years later I know The Furies Collective was a turning point as was St. Mark's a turning point. I now know many of the answers to our success rests in the penumbra of the brain, those areas we rarely see in ourselves or others, the inner life. If we can link these discoveries, psychological, to the economic, I believe we will have the basis for a strong challenge to patriarchal power. The patriarchs may not topple in our lifetime but *someone* has to brave the unknown and that is the destiny of our generation. We are the bridge generation between the desert and the promised land. If we don't build it no one gets there. Our political enemies by their colossal greed will render the earth uninhabitable. If people do not replace profit, if the land is not nourished, if simultaneity does not replace the concept of Intellectual polarization, if men do not release the "feminine" within themselves and Identify with women, if cooperation does not replace competition, generations hence will choke on blood and dust. World War II will look like a rehearsal. Our work will not be easy. The reward may be the work itself and your knowledge of the value of that work. As LaBelle sings to us, "The Revolution will not be televised." I learned that in *The Furies*.

After our break-up I saw only our failures. It took me time to realize the failure was not all our fault. It is politically impossible to create a separate, feminist "state" surrounded by an ocean of hostile patriarchs. External circumstances pulled us apart as much as we ourselves did. Most of us brokered with the outside world for menial part-time jobs to keep us alive. The clash between work and the world of the collective bore down on us. The total lack of support and outright peevishness we received from our former brothers in the New Left was no help. The ill-disguised fear of heterosexual feminists proved much harder to bear than the men's behavior. We expected more of other women. At one point the so-called radical community sunk so low as to try and pit Charlotte and myself against first, Black women and second, Black men at the Institute for Policy Studies. (We both worked there.) I am happy to report that that diseased tactic flopped.

When not working for money on our jobs we worked long hours on our political projects. We didn't sleep enough and we didn't eat enough. We tried to do everything at once partly because we were so pressured and partly because we hadn't learned to organize priorities. Even if we had known how to emotionally support one another we wouldn't have had the time to act on it.

Time has greater power than any of us imagine. As months and years rolled by I could begin to see our successes. We did go into uncharted territory. Women had not lived the way we did, not that I know of. We exposed the real divisions between us. Only by understanding those differences can we overcome them. We sparked women across the country with our newspaper and we barely knew it. Intellectually we clarified lesbianism as a political issue and we began the more difficult task of clarifying class. We provided an example, however flawed, of women who were serious about power. I believe we helped other women understand that dishonesty is the ethos of the patriarchal state. The Nixon years were not an aberration.

The test of our success is the collective members themselves. Coletta Reid went to work at Diana Press which published and printed this book. Nancy Myron worked there for 1½ years, before becoming Art Director for a D.C. firm. Ginny Berson and Jennifer Woodul along with women not in the collective founded Olivia Records. Helaine Harris and Lee Schwing started Women in Distribution. Joan Biren started a feminist filmmaking and distribution company, Moonforce Media. Sharon Deevey wrote a book called *Stat Magic* and participated in the prolonged Washington Post strike. Tasha Petersen and Susan Hathaway moved to North Carolina and I haven't heard from them since. Charlotte remains a Fellow at the Institute for Policy Studies and helped to guide *Quest* magazine which she and I founded with others. She is writing her long awaited political book this year. Kara is with her mother, Coletta. I don't know where Michelle or Cassidy are or Michelle's cat, Charly. As I write this, Baby Jesus languidly throws the completed pages on the floor because she likes to hear them rustle. Frip, one year younger, resembles a hairy hippopotamus and is happiest when eating. I wrote, so far, two novels, two books of poetry, and I'm working on another novel. I helped set up Sagaris College in 1973 then left the administration. The school did open in 1975 and I suppose it did some good but it wasn't the school I had envisioned.

The *Furies* taught me I have two talents, organizing and writing. Given the state of feminism I am in no danger of exercising the former. Goethe observed that the Germans would rather tolerate injustice than disorder. Feminists are able to tolerate both injustice and disorder. Our movement is still so far from political seriousness that we don't pay our workers a decent wage or compensate in some fashion. We devalue women's labor to the point where we expect women to work cheap or free as in Lady Bountiful. We will only succeed politically when we build structures to keep our workers alive and when we create an organization to encompass the issues which are responses to oppression. We must go one step further and develop a plan of action so we act out upon our political enemies rather than constantly reacting to our political enemies.

So that leaves me writing. Sometimes I feel as though I'm staving off disaster with a typewriter. I'm still not rich. In fact, I make less yearly than a white man who did not graduate from high school, and I have my Ph.D. Women oppression is alive and well. I'm not the only one.

Most importantly, I am no longer tied to feminism by merely conviction or ideology. I am bound by a knot I tied over time with other women. In this circle of flesh I keep fighting not because I'm brave and certainly not because I'm saintly. I fight because I am not alone and I will never be alone again. We might hurt each other, we might feel politically out on a limb sometimes but we are no longer alone. There are too many of us and we've come too far to ever turn back.

My sisters get little glory. A few enjoy or endure fame but most of them labor under the shadow of creeping poverty and without much encouragement. Over the years I've met thousands of these women. Each one is a miracle. There are thousands more I have yet to meet. But whether I know you or whether I don't, you all keep me alive and I hope that in some way I keep you alive, too. The following essays are as much a chronicle of the decade as of my own development. Off the page, in the shadows of causality, are the women who influenced me to write all this in the first place. This collection is about all of us and the life we give each other.

Violence

Is non-violence or passive resistance only effective politically if the resistors possess the ability to commit violent action? A protest gains momentum by restraint under these circumstances.

If this is true, can we expect our demonstrations, pickets and spot actions to have the same result as say the same tactic employed by the Black movement or the peace movement? No. The "establishment" considers women somewhat of a joke (including the women in that establishment). A woman nurtures, protects, complements, encourages others to carry out her ideas, etc. The possibility of women committing premeditated violence seems ludicrous. Until we threaten property or persons of the so-called establishment we will not be taken seriously. It is the ultimate perversity of our society (is it?) that a social movement is not considered a political force until it imitates the male by using force rather than reason. Once destructive potential is established then the establishment will reason with you because it is in their *self-interest* to reason with you.

Is it possible that we can create an effective new way of relating to the existing power structure by not resorting to dominance-passivity patterns?

No power group ever performed any action...no matter how beneficial to people...unless

Many of us are learning to interact with each other outside the framework of this traditional pattern but will the establishment be able to react in these non-dominating ways? Can we realistically expect these chauvinists of both sexes to deal with us or any other group without resorting to dominance-passivity patterns?

All of our demands are more than reasonable--they are the minimum requirement for a *humane* existence for *all* people. These demands have been sniggered at, ignored, belittled ad nauseum. Must we be forced into destructive acts in order to insure a bare minimum of humanity for all? (Please review the position of the Black in America before Watts and after "Burn, Baby, Burn.") Will we have utilized the ultimate corrupt tool of the chauvinist--force--or will we in fact be asserting ourselves as a physical reality via a few selective acts to illustrate our destructive potential?

I consider this one of the most painful questions we as a movement have to ask of ourselves. I have no answer and in fact, this paper is one horizontal question mark. The only statement that I can make is one all my observations have taught me:

No power group ever performs any action--no matter how beneficial to the people--unless it is in their self interest to do so.

it is in their self interest to do so.

Coitus Interruptus

Sex is used to sell everything in our country...magazines, cars, art, and *RAT.* If you packaged shit, called it Fabulous Feces and utilized a buxom woman in the advertising campaign, it would sell. All this rampant commercial sexuality is incredibly destructive. Damned if I want our bodies to sell the leprous products of our great society. Damned if I want my body to send a movement male on his butch ego trip. It's one thing if plastic people relate to each other as automatic genitalia but it's a whole other scene if we radicals and revolutionaries are a distorted version of the mass culture. Sexuality is the same whether you are a Maoist, anarchist or reconditioned Goldwaterite. The male seeks to conquer through sex while the female seeks to communicate. Put the two together and you breed hate...neither can break through the preconceived role pattern in the other. If each accepts their sexual role, even in hip terms, a cold war develops.

But despite mutual discontent with the opposite sex the male still comes out on "top." His ego can swell up like a bloated tick, gorged on his various conquests. He can parade in front of other males (whether at IBM or the SDS office) holding

For a woman to accept this defininition of herself is to accept spiritual lobotomy,

his much used prick as proof of his manhood, the locus of this identity as a male. Whoever heard of abortion mentioned in these circumstances? Notice that this parading with the typical ignorance of consequence is done for the benefit of other males.

This arid homosexuality which uses the heterosexual act as the basis for its male supremacist structure is Amerika's answer to the carnage of the Coliseum--we do it in bed spiritually instead of in the arena bodily.

To define yourself by your genitals or by a sexual act (heterosexuality, homosexuality) is to fall into the trap our sexist society has set for you. It will take men much longer to see this, to discover that sexism is political, than it will for women. Aside from the already mentioned reason that sexism is in his favor, a man can ignore sexism because his entire identity does not depend on sexual function. The boasting of conquest is demanded but he can also expect a life outside of sex--he can be a senator, a pig or big-time leader. Women are defined by sexual function alone. . in or out of the movement. The usual insensitive male response to Women's Liberation is, "All those chicks need is a good lay." We have no other identity in society or in revolutionary counter-society. Our fulfillment is still to mysteriously come via the erect penis.

For a woman to accept this definition of herself is to accept spiritual lobotomy, self-amputated before it can grow. For a woman,

self amputated before it can grow.

especially in the Women's Movement, to vocally assert her heterosexuality is to emphasize her "goodness" by her sexual activity with men. That old sexist brainwashing runs deep even into the consciousness of the most ardent feminist who will quickly tell you she loves sleeping with men. In fact, the worst thing you can call a woman in our society (again, this also applies to counter-society) is a lesbian. Women are so male-identified that they quake at the mention of this three-syllable word. The lesbian is, of course, the woman who has no need of men. When you think about it, what is so terrible about two women loving each other? To the insecure male, this is the supreme offense, the most outrageous blasphemy committed against the sacred scrotum.

After all, just what would happen if we all wound up loving each other. Good things for us, but it would mean each man would lose his personal "nigger"...a real and great loss if you are a man.

Our sexist culture destroys everyone, male and female. It prevents men from really loving anything other than themselves and what brings them pleasure (the female) and it prevents women from the exercise of self. At the root of this sexist culture is intense woman hatred and intense hatred of sexual activity. Our American emphasis on sex is a sad illustration of how false sex is and how commercial. Part of this hatred probably springs from male jealousy over female life-giving functions. Maybe some of it is due to the fact that we have more sexual staying power, especially as we mature. I can't pretend to know where it all comes from but I do know it is there. The male experience of sex is diametrically opposed to the female experience. All of our literature, (male literature, they won't publish ours yet) from

Melville to Mailer shows us this inability to enjoy sex as communication, as joy. It is either evil or an ego trip.

In line with this, the traditional male explanation for lesbianism is a patronizing use of our deepest emotions to explain their needs and fears. Men always explain lesbianism as a woman turning to another woman because she can't get a man or because she has been badly treated by men. They can't seem to cope with the fact that it is a positive response to another human being. To love another woman is an acceptance of sex which is a severe violation of the male culture (sex as exploitation) and therefore carries severe penalties. To really love another women is to communicate (at its best) and even at its worst (exotic exercise) the idea of conquest is absurd. But the problem is more varied than that. Women have been taught to abdicate the power of our bodies, both physically in athletics and self-defense and sexually. To sleep with another woman is to confront the beauty and power of your own body as well as hers. You confront the experience of your sexual self knowledge. You also confront another human being without the protective device of role. This may be too painful for most women as many have been so brutalized by heterosexual role play that they cannot begin to comprehend this real power. It is an overwhelming experience. I vulgarize it when I call it a freedom high. No wonder there is such resistance to lesbianism.

For a man to engage in a homosexual act is not the assertion of self and womanhood that it can be for a woman. It may even be a negation of self. For a man in America to love another man and express that love physically is to lose cock privilege--to become a woman in the eyes of that society (again, counter-society also)-- and he is the only male who has some idea of what it is like to be despised as a woman. Our culture is so sexist, so narrow-minded , so frightened that it can only function in terms of roles. Those roles are simplified: Male = power and dominance; female = nurturance and passivity. There is no such thing as human.

The man who wants to sleep with another man has to be a woman- it's the only way mini-minds can handle him. Those men who do manage to break through their fear of confronting their sexual experience and sleeping with another man usually find themselves torn as to who they are It is a negation of self for many. They have been so brainwashed by sexist culture that they give us the phenomenon of male homosexual promiscuity or the sadist/masochist bars, with the "masters" and "slaves"--the logic of our sexist culture carried to its ultimate end. Most male homosexuals I know are desperately clinging to the externals of cock privilege while secretly fearing they aren't really men. One of the ironies that clearly demonstrates this exists within some of the political homosexual groups--they are often male supremacist. The lesbians are not taken seriously. The more they look like traditional female sex objects, the more accepted they are.

What a pitiable comment on our generation, the males in our society closest to renouncing cock privilege, closest to breaking out of role, retreat to more restrictive roles and still cannot deal with the reality of independent womanhood, of the self-directed, non-male-identified woman. She is as much of a threat to him as to his straight brother. There are a few courageous women fighting this one out with these men, but once again women's energies are being wasted trying to educate males. Men must educate themselves, Mommy or Queen Chick isn't going to nurture anymore.

And so our sexist culture humps on its exhausted way with the Sexual Klu Klux Klan burning out the beauty in all of us. I do believe women are breaking out of and through to each other in fighting sexism. I do believe this will force the culture to re-examine itself and the backlash will be enormous. This kind of re-examination has to be done in the gut and that means concrete pain. It is a lot easier for men and male-identified women to avoid that pain by hurting people who are jeopardizing their world axis. Our very lives force people to ask questions of themselves.

I wish I could say something encouraging. I wish I could say that the irrational aspects of our beings (color, sex) will fade away in the future. I wish I could say we'd forget black and white and male and female and concentrate on being human, on being beautiful, on being alive. I wish I could say that two Fridays ago I didn't receive a phone call from a male that said, "You're Rita Mae Brown, aren't you?" "Yes," I answered. "I hear you don't like men, you're a dyke, a cunt lapper and I've put a bomb under your stairway." Click. I wish I could say that it didn't hurt.

Yale Break

Yale reeks of the rich, white man and the law school stinks of the ugliest kind, the man who upholds and defends the establishment or at best tries to reform it through its courts of "justice." Here in this hotbed of privilege one of the most exciting Women's Liberation Conferences to date was conducted between February 27 and March 1, 1970. Maybe we subconsciously realized we were in the heart of the polite pig structure but whatever it was we drew together.

It started out as do most conferences with an obligatory panel song and dance number. Yale had managed to secure two star performers for the bill, Kate Millet and Naomi Weisstein. Kate spoke first and in true academic fashion she worked her show. I detest that method but I can in no way argue with the content of that performance. Her insights are extremely valuable, incisive and penetrating. To condense or paraphrase them would be doing Kate Millet an injustice. Naomi Weisstein's approach was very personalized and intimate. When she finished she was no longer a star but a flesh and blood woman and we knew we could touch her. She received a standing ovation of such duration that we all got high off the noise. Even the two women

We spoke from inside and we laughed from inside also.

behind me who were putting both women down throughout the whole evening with comments like, "I wonder if she's married, she's not very pretty."--even those two got on their feet. Naomi hit home.

What wonders me (to use an ethnic phrase) is why do these two women want to work within the academic structure at all? They are so obviously superior to any of the dry rot found within the ivory towers of penultimate time. To even think of working within the university system is blatantly reformist. Why waste precious energies on a corrupt and corrupting structure? Why don't women like Kate Millet and Naomi Weisstein come together and form a learning collective--not a university, not an imitation of the amoral, antagonistic male structure but a real, living place where we can come together and learn from each other? A place where learning is creation and a joy to be shared. I have a lot to learn from these women but I also think they have a lot to learn from me. That goes for every woman I know. A learning collective would mean an enormous expenditure of energy and dedication in the beginning on the part of a few women but it is the kind of challenge we should rise up to meet--especially our sisters floundering within the alien, university system. Those of us who left the university before it destroyed our heads will come together to help, also.

That such a move is both possible and productive was foreshadowed at the Yale Conference on the next day, workshop day. The topics were arranged around the usual heterosexual priorities but there was enough flexibility so that the workshop participants could form their own direction. The Life Style workshop offers a good example of what happened at Yale and what might work for a learning collective. The room was crowded (maybe 70 women) and the Yale women simply began the group process by stating the life styles available, skirting homosexuality, of course. From that point women began to participate and share their experiences and their analyses from those experiences. Those of us from the newly formed Sappho Collective were given an opportunity after initial hedging (like an hour's worth) to talk about other kinds of life styles. The honesty level was high and each of us began to open up. Soon the women in the workshop stopped their desiccated intellectual trips and began to talk from the gut. Women began to take each other in as total human beings, the typical male forms of judgment and disapproval were suspended. There was a feeling of warmth, of response and of communication--and also of playfulness. The lightness was due in part to a remarkable woman whom I will call Lady Teazle to protect her from the male heterosexual capitalists who buy her brain and also because her conduct was slightly scandalous by heterosexual standards. To the Sappho Collective she was a roaring camp. Halfway through the workshop she put her hands on her hips and fired, "Listen, Mary, I've been sitting here tolerating the dreariness and it only fortifies my conclusion that heterosexuality is a myth. Women and men don't really like each other at all--they just bump their uglies, so to speak." She followed this statement with delicate blasts at the institution of heterosexuality until when the smoke had cleared so had heterosexuality. After Lady Teazle had finished, a great portion of the room had witnessed the demolition of one of their forms of oppression--at least by humor, if nothing else. This woman's approach helped to humanize the situation and turned the workshop into a moving experience. We got away from the heavy, heavy political raps where words replace fists and sentence structure masquerades as reality. We spoke from inside and we laughed from inside also. I would think that that is a turning point for women, a good starting point for a learning collective, and a vital step toward revolution.

Something About "Walk a Mile in My Shoes"

Fifteen women lined up at the corner of the Yale law school on February 27, 1970 and actively terrorized males on the campus. The action was spontaneously led by Carla, Jennifer, and Marchoff of Vassar and the mysterious Lady Teazle. The passersby were given a little sample of the street chatter we women hear every day of our lives. The reactions of the "assaulted" men ranged from shocked disbelief to real fear. One of Lady Teazle's more inventive tactics was to allow a male to walk by until he got smack in the middle of the line and then surround him. We were, in a sense, playing, but the men did not see the humor in it and a few were hostile. It only illustrated to me, at least, that no male in America wants to be in the position of a woman (dehumanized sex object) for even two minutes. Our little guerilla action did just that--put him in our shoes. He couldn't wait to kick them off. Being treated as a woman is the worst thing that can happen to a man.

By Saturday the word of Operation Hassle had spread so that more women joined us in our heady conquest of the law school corner. Many of the men must have gotten the word too because as soon as one would see us he would scurry to the opposite

Being treated as a woman is the worst thing that can happen to a man.

side of the street--does that ring a familiar bell? After about twenty minutes of commanding a by now strangely emptied street we headed toward the local ptomaine pits. About a block away Lady Teazle looked over her shoulder and remarked that the corner had become populated once more. Anyone got any ideas--like 2000 of us on the corner of 42nd and Broadway?

Say It Isn't So

Female Liberation in Boston has long contained some of my favorite people in the movement. In November 1969 at the Congress to Unite Women the New York radicals fought side by side with our Boston sisters to cut through some of the NOW bullshit. We felt good about each other and when ten of us went up there over the Washington's Birthday weekend, we were elated. Our joy was short-lived.

Saturday night, Female Liberation presented a panel discussion that divided between Marlene Dixon's endless rap on women's history and Roxanne Dunbar. That in itself was pretty demoralizing. Ms. Dixon was at the podium entirely too long. Although our patience was strained by the length of her delivery, our spirits began to shred when we recognized that old professorial delivery, so popular among males in our academic whorehouses. I don't like to be talked at. That whole let-me-tell-you-something approach reeks of male identification. But in all fairness to Ms. Dixon, she may not have had time to discover new ways to transmit information. And isn't it part of our oppression that when given a chance we will imitate the male?

If...the fact that we see each other as men have taught us to see.

Sitting in the big hall, obviously bored beyond belief, my eyes began to travel the obese gilt framed pictures of our founding fathers. There was Admiral Preble, whoever the hell he was, and Samuel Choate, George Washington and John Quincy Adams. And behind the mothers of monotonous monologue there was the largest, most god-awful picture of Daniel Webster on the floor of the Senate...body poised in a heroic tremble, arm thrust forward and mouth open. It was his famous "Liberty and Union, now and forever" address. Just in case people couldn't identify this stirring scene, underneath the picture in large gold letters was "Liberty and Union, now and forever." Above the senators, like a chorus of imprisoned angels, sat the women--all in bonnets, all neatly attentive to the goings on below. What shit, I thought. What real, visible shit. At this point the speakers had somewhat quieted themselves and asked for audience participation. I shot my mouth off with the following:

Sitting here in this room, looking at all the pictures of rich white men and simultaneously listening (I listened a little bit) to your rap on women's history, things begin to have a new perspective. Look at the picture behind you--we are still in the gallery and not on the floor like those women. It seems very clear to me that no woman in this room is bound by laws made by dead men, made when none of us had a voice in government...laws still preserved by rich white men today. To hell with those rich white men. They are polluting our environment and poisoning our souls. Our struggle is against the male power system which is a system of war and death. If in the process of that struggle we are forced to mutilate, murder and massacre those men, then so it must be. But simultaneous with that struggle we must also struggle to build a culture of life and love. We must respect and love each other. To date, the women's movement has consistently rejected women who are trying to build a new way of life, a life of loving other women. If we can't love each other, if we can't learn to grow together, then we will only have a rebellion against the male death culture--a rebellion which may be successful. But I think we are capable of revolution. To love without role, without power plays, is revolution. I believe these are our goals.

This was followed by applause from the audience and stunned disbelief from the panel. Ms Dixon piokod up on the struggle against the death culture. Roxanne Dunbar also commented on the battle lines. This was followed by an embarrassing silence. Questions were then hurriedly solicited. Forty-five minutes later, Cynthia Sun stood up and in a low, controlled voice repeated painfully:

I'm tired of hearing about the oppression of women. I'm tired of hearing a slick public relations rap that doesn't come from the gut. Let's look at the oppression right here in this room. You women on the panel have used your heterosexual privilege to silence the topic of love especially since that topic was love between women, which would seem to me to be critical to the movement.

Another stunned silence. Marlene Dixon allowed as how some of her best friends were homosexual. At this point a woman two rows in front of us exploded with, "She said it! She actually said it!" Laughter. Roxanne evaded the question again and again until I yelled, "Your silence is oppressive. Why do you oppress us?" Then she delivered what will always be in my mind one of the most incredible raps I've ever heard. "Sexuality is not the key issue. What I want to do is get women out of bed. Women can love each other but they don't have to sleep together. I think that homosexuality is a chosen oppression whereas being a woman is the root oppression. I don't think it's that important.''

What we all want to do is get women out of bed. Sexuality is the key of our oppression. We are continually seen in sexual terms, we are defined by our genitals as brutally as a non-white is defined by pigment, be it red, yellow, black or brown. To ignore the issue of women loving other women, to label it lesbianism and divisive, is to turn around and define me and all my sisters in the same manner in which women are defined by men, by my sexual activity and function. The only way we are going to get ourselves out of the bed is to see each other as human beings. The entire Haymarket chaos was a vivid illustration of the fact that we see each other as men have taught us to see. One of the panel said lesbianism isn't an issue unless you wear a neon sign. Can anything more precisely illustrate how we oppress each other? Why is fighting to have your oppression recognized and dealt with, wearing a neon sign? In other words, no one will know you are homosexual unless you tell. Bullshit, sisters. One doesn't get liberated by hiding. One doesn't possess integrity by passing for ''white.'' We are trying against all odds--from the male culture and from our ''sisters'' in the Women's Liberation movement--to develop a life style where there are no roles, where there are no power plays, where a human being is a human being and not a collage of male-identified, half-smashed roles.

After the meeting, women in the audience came up to us. Many realized for the first time how women tear each other apart. Many who had never given the issue a first thought identified with our rage. One young woman said, "I don't know what I am. But I do know shit when I see it and they really shit on you."

Another woman mentioned that it was absurd to try to divide oppression between lesbian and woman's oppression as the two are solidly intertwined. One woman simply said, "Thank you," hugged us and hurried out.

As we went down the long, steep steps to the road we talked among ourselves about how class split the old feminist movement. Our movement is splitting over the "lesbian" issue, or more precisely, women's oppression of other women. We must deal with this in a constructive way or we will be at each other's throats just as we were in Boston. For a moment, I thought I heard the rustle of our skirts. Over one hundred years ago a meeting of abolitionists was threatened by a mob of angry, violent white men. One of the men who was an abolitionist escaped through the window and the hall was filled with trapped women. At that time, each white woman took the hand of a black woman and calmly walked down that same row of long, long steps through the mob--their courage earned them a safe passage. I looked around at my "lesbian" sisters and realized we were quite alone--the Female Liberationists had exited out the side doors.

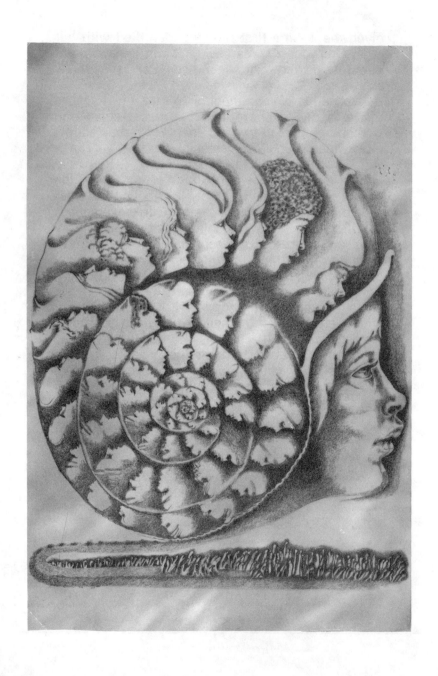

August 26, 1970, N.Y.C.

Fifth Avenue was filled with fifty thousand women at 5:30 p.m. on August 26, 1970. The newspapers gave conservative estimates of around 6,000. Well, what can you expect from the white man's media? If you had been standing on the corner of 42nd Street and Fifth Avenue you would have seen one solid mile of women. That sight alone must have chilled the heart of the hottest chauvinist. Thirty thousand women marched down Fifth Avenue for the vote in 1913. Here we are again, a new and energetic movement on the avenue once more, this time for equal rights. Here we are again committing the same mistakes our grandmothers did fifty years ago.

The suffragist movement was dominated by wealthy and middle class women and so its goals were understandably the goals of wealthy and middle class women. Revolution was not the issue. The issue was gaining some power in the white man's government. Once we possessed the vote it became painfully clear that we possessed little else. We couldn't really run for office except for a few states that let us by. The male establishment was busy digging up moldering blue laws to keep us away from the reins of imperialist government. But

Thirty thousand women marched down Fifth Ave. in 1913.

our grandmothers had risked a great deal to get us the vote, why couldn't they push one step further and get us equal rights?

Our struggle had been battled in one form or another since Abigail Adams warned her husband concerning women's rights way back during the Constitutional Convention. It had taken generations to get this far and many women were tired. They had picked up the banner from their mothers and had spent a lifetime fighting for suffrage. Many had focused only on the vote and when it was granted in 1920 they thought the objective reached. The more farsighted wing of the movement regrouped around the National Woman's Party at 144 Constitution Avenue in Washington, D.C. These women pushed for an Equal Rights Amendment and Alice Paul, now in her eighties, is still at 144 Constitution Avenue fighting for the amendment. The suffrage movement was exhausted, fragmented and drenched in class ignorance. The momentum was spent and only a handful of women like Miss Paul were left to carry on. But today, the issue of equal rights is a reformist issue rather than radical, and it is a reformist issue to the distinct disadvantage of working class women. If our middle class sisters succeed in getting the amendment passed it will be at the expense of other women.

Perhaps this can be seen more clearly if we view the issue through the eyes of the existing government. In May of 1969 a group of women from N.O.W. visited Patricia Hitt in her offices at the Health, Education and Welfare Building. After much bombast concerning the unrest of American women with tokenism, Betty Friedan told Mrs. Hitt point-blank that the Equal Rights Amendment would be "a cheap way to buy off American women." Mrs. Hitt was to transmit this analysis to

President Nixon. Apparently she did. Mrs. Friedan was dead center when she assessed the value of the Equal Rights Amendment to the present administration. Being a clever politician, she translated the amendment into terms that spelled benefit to the white male government. Of course, she wants the amendment because of what it can do for middle class women as well as what it can do for her hoped-for political career. But the die was cast. The amendment is to defuse the revolutionary wing of the Women's Liberation Movement and to open vistas of establishment opportunity for professional women. It's very simple. With the amendment passed and ratified, women of the middle class will concentrate on furthering their own status and neglect the "dangerous" issues the revolutionaries have raised. These women do not begin to question the basic structure of our nation, they are gaining too many benefits from Wall Street and its colonies. Even when child care centers and abortion clinics are established across the land, the country will not be shaken. It will free more women to work for more rich men who can then exploit more poor people here and abroad. More women, especially white heterosexual women, will be siphoned off into the profits and before you know it, women will become as proficient at exploitation as men. Money talks. You dig?

Another aspect of this amendment is that its passage signals the suspension of all protective legislation. At least that's what Attorney General Mitchell has stated. Credibility should be attached to male statements only when those statements refer to punitive actions to be taken against women. In that case, Mitchell is telling the truth. (Washington is full of surprises.) The removal of protective legislation will not affect editors, magazine writers and public relations women, but it will affect factory workers or to put it more clearly, working class women of all races.

Working class women have neither the time nor the resources to fight their exploitation in the white man's courts. Cleanliness laws, lunch hours, safety measures, work hour limitations, minimum wages, premium pay for overtime, weight-lifting regulations will all be wiped off the books. Since only 15% of the women workers are unionized the prospect of quickly righting these wrongs doesn't look promising. Given the male leadership of most unions it looks impossible.

The middle class women pushing for the Equal Rights Amendment have not addressed themselves to the problem of protective legislation for women workers. Their class privilege makes them blind to even a superficial recognition of the interests of oppressed women. The point is not the protective legislation per se, but the absence of consciousness in middle class women regarding other women's lives and livelihoods.

If this amendment passes it will succeed in splitting women along class lines. The amendment will probably pass. A few white male leaders will make ridiculous and/or chivalric statements concerning the amendment and sweet femininity but the tide has turned. Even Emmanuel Cellar, reigning turd over the House Judiciary Committee is being forced to give ground . . . Cellar has held the amendment up in his committee for decades with the intelligent declaration that it will get out of his committee "over my dead body." Perhaps he is giving ground due to an unpublicized terminal disease (such as galloping deterioration of the brain cells), but more than likely he is giving ground because larger pieces of system excrement than himself are pressuring him. Given these exhilarating facts, is there any way out?

An obvious alternative is for middle class women to give up their privileges and join less privileged women so we can fight white male exploitation together. But how many people do you know who have given up their privileges lately? If working class women, Third World women and lesbians organize to educate middle class women some of those women might join the struggle. It should be stressed that most middle class women are working out of an absence of class consciousness *not* out of malicious class hatred. Saying that middle class women need a consciousness of how they oppress other women is not as easy as helping them gain it. The American middle class is famous for its hostility to any concept of how they might be damaging other people. It took Blacks three hundred years to drum the idea of racial prejudice and its effects into white middle class heads--some still haven't gotten the message.

One hope lies in the fact that all women, regardless of race, class and sexual preference, are treated as less than full blown persons every day in their lives. The forms this takes varies with race, class and sexual preference, but the corroding effects on the psyche are the same: anger, frustration on one end and despair and hopelessness on the other. Many women attempt to alleviate the damage by throwing themselves into "acceptable" pursuits. If this recognition can be transmitted to the middle class women some might renounce their privileges over other women.

However, if middle class women continue to exercise their privileges with full knowledge of how this oppresses other women, those middle class women are doomed to share the fate of the existing power structure. When non-white women, lesbians and working class women rise up against oppressors those oppressors will be swept away.

Perhaps the clearest illustration of the existing problem and its future solution can be seen in the events on August 26th in New York City:

At 11:00 AM N.O.W. picketed the Stock Exchange and then went to lunch at White's, a chic male restaurant in the area. At 1:00 PM they filed into Battery Park and made speeches thereby insuring that they would miss the working class women of the area, who lunch from 12 to 1.

As the Stock Exchange Stormtroopers sat down to sweet repast amid male gastronomic reaction a far more significant event was taking place at Willy's, another eatery. The waitresses had heard that August 26th was to be a Woman's Strike. Strike to working class women means action. These waitresses on their own initiative sat down on the job at the height of rush hour and refused to serve the fat cats. Since the women were sitting in the same room with the ravenous market rapists it was a highly charged scene. Our sisters demanded higher wages. They received no protection in this action as they have no union, furthermore they didn't ask support from Women's Liberation nor did they seek publicity. Finally they did serve the men but their point was made, when the worker on the bottom of the heap refuses to work, the system totters quickly. The worker on the bottom of the heap is a woman. To date no information has been received as to whether the waitresses have been fired for their spirited action.

Working class women tuned in to publicity their middle class sisters so carefully sought after, and the working class women interpreted the strike in their own direction and devastating way to suit their own needs. In New Jersey a grandmother (name withheld by request) was watching the news coverage of the day and saw a poster that said, "Starve a Rat Today." She turned to her long-time spouse and declared her cooking days were over and he could damn well cook for her. A protest from her long-time exploiter was answered with a fist on the table and "Liberation or separation!" He cooked and he's cooking still.

Reports filtered in through telephones and by word of mouth of women demanding the labor be shared. One man in Pennsylvania came home to find a suitcase packed with all his belongings sitting on the front step. The sister had decided to break her chains rather than burnish them.

Wall Street was the scene of more activity when a group of women leafleted the office workers to unionize. The leafleting was planned as an alternative action to all the middle class pomp and circumstance. These few women have been working for months, a few for years, to help close the class gap. In desperation they have been forced to stop beating their brains out trying to educate middle class women and they have begun to organize working class women. These women and a handful of other groups, among them the Third World women and the lesbians, have been the only elements in New York City willing to tackle the problem. There were no T.V. cameras on Wall St. and Nassau, no crowds of well-dressed women singing, "Liberation Now"...there were hurried exchanges with file clerks and secretaries afraid of losing their jobs. There were hostile and obscene comments from men--yes, those same austere financiers tend to drop the mask of respectability when it comes to women unionizing their "shops."

The organizers at Wall St. knew better than to ask for support from the glamour elements of the movement. All the cameras and well-dressed women showed up on Fifth Avenue and marched down to Bryant Park. There the thousands cheered to the strains of Betty Friedan's, "we want to walk hand in hand with men." Gloria Steinem and Kate Millet gave speeches of love and sisterhood. The women were enthusiastic. The only jarring note was when a lesbian grabbed the microphone after being discouraged by the heavies. She told the crowd to stand behind their lesbian sisters who were being arrested and harrassed for no reason at all--except of course, that they are lesbians. And the show went on. No cheers for the Wall Street workers, no cheers for the Black sisters thrown into jails, no cheers for the lesbians beaten senseless on the streets. The cheers were all for a future of projected goodies and for that old Equal Rights Amendment, the bandaid to heal the gaping, festering wound of rich, white, American male politics.

But the cheers have stirred new women... women who won't make a mockery of the word Liberation...women who trust deeds not the promise of them...poor women, Black women, Puerto Rican women, Asian-American women, working women and women who love their sisters...women who will bypass rhetoric and make a revolution.

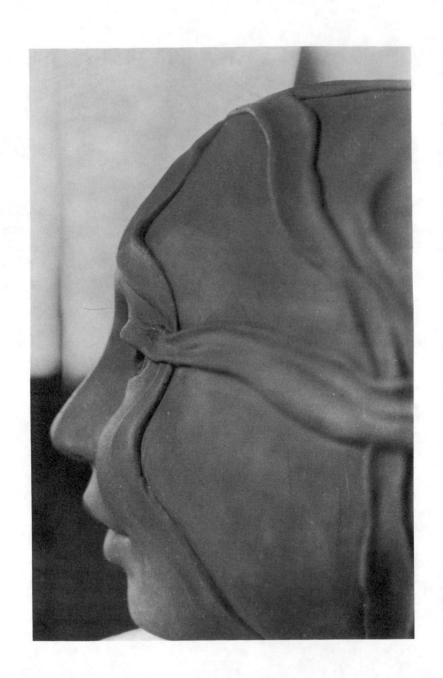

Hanoi to Hoboken: a round trip ticket

Why the persistent enthusiasm for far-away places and distant struggles with imperialism? Why travel to Hanoi when you can go to Hoboken and see the same show? Granted the costumes are native, the accents, New Jersey, the exotic touch is missing and you won't get napalm for an encore but the plot is still the same: Oppression.

There are a number of reasons why Hanoi fascinates so many women in our movement and why Hoboken is definitely a drag. Visiting Hanoi or Havana and writing articles on such a visit is one way to legitimatize our movement through participation in those areas that the white, middle class, male left movement has designated as legitimate. It shows that we women are reaching out beyond what the male left defines as "Women's issues" to what they define as the "important" issues. Women's issues are not important. It is inconceivable to think of a male left heavy going to Hoboken to study how lack of child care facilities oppresses poor women.

I am not for one minute announcing that U.S. imperialism is not a concern of the Women's Liberation Movement. The struggle of our Vietnamese sisters is anything but frivolous, but the

Together. . .goes structured disciplined consciousness raising.

way in which many American women approach that struggle is both imitative and frivolous.

When our Vietnamese sisters throw out the invader they will have yet another war on their hands, the war against sexism in their own society. But right now those women are fighting for their lives. Here in Amerika many women are also fighting for their lives, there are no bombers but the struggle is just as relentless and deadly—we are the poor, the Black, the Latin and the Lesbian. We aren't exotic and we aren't remotely glamorous. The male left is not concerned with us although it will make token statements for the benefit of Black males concerning racism (the Black woman is supposedly incorporated in the Black male). By flying to Hanoi, you win attention of the male left. By working in Hoboken you attract no attention at all and by working with Lesbians you are quickly dismissed as irrelevant and sick.

Another reason why Hanoi is such a beacon for revolutionary moths: you can return to the U.S. and rip off the liberals with speaking tours, books, movies, etc., on your experiences there. That's not to say that all who go to Hanoi are rip-offs, nor are all who go eager for male left approval, but enough are to make it a problem. Unfortunately, poverty and woman oppression are not so lucrative a profession despite recent attempts by the establishment media to cash in on these oppressions.

If you worked in Hoboken, who would be grateful but the women in Hoboken--women who have no power, prestige or money to bestow on anyone.

What I am getting at is this: It's easier to worry about far-away problems than our problems here at home. Not only is it easy, it's comfortable because the problems here at home might possibly be cleared up if we worked at clearing them up. How far would Ho Chi Minh have gotten if he had run all over the globe to witness other forms of imperialism? By concentrating on imperialism abroad we use quantities of energy that could be used here, like setting up health clinics. In other words, the priorities of the anti-imperialist women are ass-backwards. For example, *off our backs,* a feminist newspaper, ran a special issue on Women and Imperialism on December 31, 1970. Most issues of this paper (after the initial six issues) carry some article on the subject of women and imperialism. Has there been a special issue on Lesbianism? Articles in most issues? Plain, flat, ugly, No. What about Black women? Latin women? Poor women? It's not fair to single out *off our backs,* most of the other papers and magazines are the same. Our feminist media is young and wobbly and because of that many of the articles in the big city papers such as *oob* and *Rat* have been in those areas that male politics has considered important. The other papers and magazines not contaminated by male left politics confined themselves to heterosexual interests. The media is simply a reflection of the white, middle class, straight bias of the Women's Liberation Movement itself.

Imperialism begins at home. The best place to fight imperialism is at its center. Let's stab the monster in its heart rather than slapping its fingers.

Imperialism, racism and the attendant disregard for human life (change that to all forms of life) spring from sexism. Way back in the dim mists of prehistory when man beat down, degraded and enslaved women he clearly showed his career preferences. In degrading women he degraded himself. Once the initial inhumanity was committed it was a simple matter to progress step by step to today. History is man remembering the subsequent degradations of other men over time. He degraded us at such an early age that he has practically forgotten it and derives little satisfaction from it in a political sense although he gets a great deal out of it personally. The real glory is in shitting on other men. To fight The Man we don't need to go to Hanoi, we fight him right here.

Let's be clear in our priorities ideologically (pragmatics will follow later in the paper) and focus our energies on the destruction of sexism rather than scatter our energies all over the globe on the latter stages of sexism known as imperialism. By fighting here, which is the current international center of the latter stages of sexism known as imperialism, we help our Vietnamese sisters. Any attention we can draw away from our sisters gives them more time to breathe. In practical terms, we cannot do more. We cannot launch an armada to join them in combat. We can express solidarity, which we have done, and we can do our best to keep in communication with our Vietnamese sisters, relating their experiences and struggle to American women and vice versa.

It does us and the Vietnamese women no good if we join the male left in desultory protest. Women have tried that for a number of years and the government's response is the dreary, well known, no response. Uncle Sam knows how to ward off anti-imperialists, after all he's had nearly 200 years experience. But he's not so ready for anti-sexists. While he's got his arms up fighting the NLF abroad and protestors at home, let's grab him in the crotch and make him howl.

Vietnamese women understand that howl. They told Charlotte Bunch when she visited Viet

Nam in 1970 that Amerikan women must exercise power. The cruel irony is that the Vietnamese women take us more seriously than we take ourselves. And isn't that the key to women oppression: We have Internalized The Man's definition of women and do not take ourselves seriously. Neither do we take other women seriously so we shit on the Lesbian who in many cases does take other women seriously. We write a lot and we talk a lot and we cry a lot. Unless I am completely without perception, I don't think writing, talking and crying have yet produced a mass movement of political power.

I'd like to present what I believe are the first steps to political power. Since I am only one woman I can hardly present this as a comprehensive program in the first phase of our revolution. If this remains my idea then it isn't even a first step, it's a retreat from responsibility. If the ideas spark further ideas in your head and you share it and build with other women, then we will all get somewhere.
I: *WORK PROJECTS*

Women with economic privilege, whether straight or lesbian, Black or white or Latin, should organize to meet the survival needs of women without economic privilege. This means food distribution centers, child care centers, health care centers, self-defense programs and halfway houses for women in transition or without adequate housing. If you have special skills such as editorial abilities, mechanical or medical knowledge, anything, set up a teaching program and share it. These projects will take time and work as well as patience and understanding with yourself. The women whose needs you will be meeting may have no feminist consciousness at all. Don't look down on them. It's hard to have consciousness of anything when you are hungry. You will need a great deal of patience with yourself to really get in touch with this kind of oppression and why you have ignored it in the past.

Together with these work projects goes structured, disciplined consciousness raising. This process helps women get in touch with their distinctive oppression. The Black woman learns to understand racism in a political sense rather than just in a personal sense. She can begin to see the intimate connection between racism and sexism through testimony with her sisters. The Lesbian recognizes Lesbian oppression from the male culture and from heterosexual women. She begins to understand how this supposed individual trait, choice of sex partner and life style, is an attack on the Amerikan political structure. And so it goes, each woman learns from another woman how her particular life is a reflection of and a response to the dominant, white, rich, male culture and after that the sub-culture she herself lives in. Each woman learns that her life is a political life and by examining that life each woman learns the mechanics of oppression. Once you know how something works you can begin to fix it or fight it.

II: *RE-EDUCATION*

This is partly done through consciousness-raising but it must be transmitted on a large scale through the feminist media. If we are serious in our work, we can only trust our own feminist media and we can relate only to that media. That media needs to be expanded. Each city needs its own newspaper. We also need other forms of media--films, slide shows, music, etc. If you start a paper, concentrate on your locality. Local news is immediate. Women can identify with what happens in their own city and in the lives of people like themselves. Be local and serve the needs of your women if you want to touch their lives. If you carry articles of international feminist events, be sure to help your readers see how this affects their own lives.

III: *LESBIANISM*

Before our movement can advance as a political force with a coherent women's ideology (not something borrowed from the male left) we need to completely analyze Lesbianism. This is the touchstone of our self-Image, the mirror of our oppression and is such an intense experience that it cuts across racial and class barriers. Living communes hinge on this issue as does all subsequent feminist analysis of sexism.

Lesbianism is the one issue that deals with women responding positively to other women as total human beings worthy of total commitment. It is the one area where no male can tread. It is also the one area that demands deep self-criticism. To hide from this question is to hide from yourself. To hide from this question Is to doom the movement to a pale Imitation of existing leftist Ideologies--ideologies that may have served the needs of dedicated men in Russia in 1897, in China in the 40's, but which cannot and do not serve the needs of women today.

Lesbianism Is important structurally because confronting it will help us develop differences. Every woman can confront the issue of Lesbianism because she has the potential to be a Lesbian. It is more difficult to confront class and racial differences because there is not that commonality. One does not transcend race and class--you can only come to a clear understanding of those differences in your own life and then use that understanding in conjunction with women from different classes and races to build a solid politics. Lesbianism is the great gut issue, it touches every one of us. If we learn how to deal with such an explosive issue constructively (which we are in the process of doing) then we will have the tools to deal with the other two explosive issues: Race and Class. Lesbianism will provide us with the individual and group skills for constructive confrontation, for struggle, for progress. In other words, we need a foundation to build our house upon and this issue gives us our ideological and technical foundation. We cannot unify unless we deal with this issue first.

Those three steps make up what I see as the first phase toward seriousness and toward real change in the lives of all women. Many of us can see beyond this first phase, but we must accomplish these goals before we can move on. They aren't easy goals, maybe that's why we are tempted to concentrate on distant places. The first step involves nothing less than meeting the survival needs of all women. But we must do this or the Women's Liberation Movement is destined to stay a white, middle class, heterosexual movement-- physically and psychically. If you want to see what comes of that, visit the Women's Party at 144 Constitution Ave., Washington, D.C., the grave-yard and the shrine of the last great wave of white, middle class, heterosexual feminism.

To advocate other goals at this time, like worldwide revolution is to slip from the serious and pragmatic to the imagined and fantastic. We can have women united across the globe but we must start somewhere and that somewhere is with the abovementioned measures, unglamorous though they may be. If we do not commit ourselves to this serious work, if we indulge ourselves in "right on" rhetoric, we create a preposterous lie and its twin, cynicism. The only people capable of living with that kind of unreality will be our self-ordained leaders who have need of the illusion to inflate the ego, who have need of the liturgy for a grim, old form revolution and its heavy death wish. We must begin to achieve concrete results with our energy or we will, as a movement, lapse into disbelief in our own capabilities and our political effectiveness will be limited to a few, self-indulgent media stars trotted out by the male establishment in an orgy of tokenism.

We must begin to achieve these concrete ends in order to test ourselves. We will learn a great deal from these early projects--self-reliance, pride and organizational skills. If the management of the state were in our hands tomorrow we would not be ready for it. We must train to handle political responsibility for our own lives and other lives through these kinds of outreach projects. You learn by doing it. Do it. We will all do it together. This first step is the hardest because we have so few models or examples for it, another reason why it is so crucial.

So we have a lot to learn from a visit to Hanoi, we learn we have to come home to Hoboken. Let's take ourselves seriously and seriously support our sisters in Viet Nam who do believe in us. Let's begin the slow and tedious labor here in our own backyard that will eventually change the world.

Living With Other Women

It is the primacy of women relating to women, of women creating a new consciousness of and with each other which is at the heart of women's liberation, and the basis for the cultural revolution. Together we must find, reinforce and validate our authentic selves. As we do this, we confirm in each other that struggling incipient sense of pride and strength, the divisive barriers begin to melt, we feel this growing solidarity with our sisters. We see ourselves as prime, find our centers inside of ourselves. We find receding the sense of alienation, of being cut off, of being behind a locked window, of being unable to get out what we know is inside. We feel a real-ness, feel at last we are coinciding with ourselves. With that real self, with that consciousness, we begin a revolution to end the imposition of all coercive identifications, and to achieve maximum autonomy in human expression.

from The Woman-Identified-Woman

Before the dawn of the woman-identified-woman, back in the Age of Spermatic Oppression, women did love and live with other women. Two women met, fell in love, married and lived ever

. . .coinciding with ourselves.

after. The women were forced to lead a double life if they were to economically and socially survive. It was a high price to pay but countless women paid it and are paying it still because life with another women allows greater freedom for self-knowledge and far more emotional support. This kind of life, which I will call old gay, is another version of that great Amerikan lie, the Individual Solution. The Individual Solution means that you and your lover can stay aloof from the problems of others, work hard, save your money, budget wisely and lead the "good life". Lesbians had no choice in staying away from the problems of other people, they were never welcome. For old gay women the Individual Solution was the only road for them. Along with the lie of the Individual Solution hung the albatross of love oppression. Women of the pre-woman identified woman era were love drugged. Love was the answer. It solved all problems and if allowed to flow free it could solve the problems of the world. All a woman had to do was find that four letter word, love, and that other four letter word, life, just opened up and bloomed with eternal joy. Of course, you had to work to make love work--it was your life's work. Old gay women were just as oppressed by the love definition applied to women as heterosexual women because the definition makes women into a function (lover, comforter, companion) rather than a person. Since women were neither seen nor treated as persons, as full-fledged individuals, few women had a sense of self but only a sense of function.

Lesbians, although more independent by virtue of being free from a man, had internalized along with love oppression many other values of the establishment, and these were reflected in how they lived. For instance, old gay, like other forms of oppression, imitated the values of the dominant culture (the white, rich, heterosexual male) with few improvements. Class and race lines were more fluid but the standard was that of materialism and status within the system. In other words, you could move "up" much more easily in the old gay world than in the straight world but the values were much the same. Women who were married set up house together. Women who were unattached continued to look for someone to love and marry. It was all conducted underground so there was a taste of excitement to it and if you lived in one of the big cities, a taste of glamor. But it was the same pattern as the rest of society where you isolate yourself from others who share your oppression and try to "make it" on your own or in tandem.

Before the Women's Liberation Movement, old gay lesbians had organized into the Daughters of Bilitis. This nationwide organization did not and does not have radical politics. Its purpose was to promote greater understanding of the lesbian way of life, and hopefully, to allow lesbians to participate in the mainstream of society. In the late 1960's as Women's Liberation began to gather strength many old gay women became interested in the movement but remained outside it because of the theme of this issue: How we live and with whom. Old gay women knew from bitter experience that heterosexual women neither understood the lesbian living situation nor desired to understand it. The heterosexual women had accepted the male definition of women to such an extent that the idea of a woman living with and loving another woman was too threatening even though there was similarity in how they both lived. The early movement blatantly discriminated against the lesbian, in some cases expelling women who were lesbians. A few women refused to be repulsed. At the same time other old gay women helped found and shape the Gay Liberation Movement. As the lesbians in Women's Liberation became increasingly dissatisfied over their treatment at the hands of heterosexual women, the lesbians in Gay Liberation became dissatisfied with their treatment at the hands of homosexual men. These women came together and tried to define what had been their lives and what their lives were now becoming due to some heavy changes in consciousness. Their effort became the paper, *The Woman-Identified-Woman.*

Woman-Identified Woman moved beyond the definition of old gay and the traditional definition of women toward a concept of women defining themselves. It sounds so simple and it is; yet, women are just beginning to define themselves. A woman-identified woman is one who defines herself in relationship to other women and most importantly as a self apart and distinct from other selves, not with function as the center of self, but being. In other words, only you can identify yourself; only you know who you are. As long as you accept male values you cannot accept yourself. The entire Women's Liberation Movement has proved time and time again that those values never granted woman a self, only a service. A woman can best find out who she is with other women, not with just one other woman but with other women, who are also struggling to free themselves from an alien and destructive culture. It is this new concept, that of woman-identified woman, that sounds the death knell for the male culture and calls for a new culture where cooperation, life and love are the guiding forces of organization rather than competition, power and bloodshed. This concept will change the way we live and who we live with.

The women who wrote *Woman-Identified*

Woman and the women who have come to understand it are in a transition period. We must move out of our old living patterns and into new ones. Those of us who believe in this concept must begin to build collectives where women are committed to other women on all levels--emotional, physical, economic and political. Monogamy can be cast aside, no one will "belong" to another. Instead of being shut off from each other in overpriced cubicles we can be together, sharing the shitwork as well as the highs. Together we can go through the pain and liberation of curing the diseases we have all contracted in the world of male dominance, imperialism and death. Women-identified collectives are nothing less than the next step towards a Women's Revolution.

None of us are there yet. Few of us are even in collectives much less woman-identified collectives. But at least we know what has to be done. This time of transition is a time of reaching out in the dark and hoping another sister's hand will reach back and connect. Knowing what has to be done makes it harder in some ways as we are more impatient for the collectives to materialize. It can be a time of anguish because we may be ready to try to build a woman-identified collective and find that no one else is ready to build with us. A collective, like a revolution, cannot be built by one woman. But it will come to pass. And when it does we will look back on our various lives as some old discarded rocket boosters and fully realize just how much we were compromised and strung out by a very basic matter: How we live and with whom.

Take a Lesbian to Lunch

Women's tragedy is that we are not defeated by hubris, gods or our own passion but by society; a society controlled by insensitive, rich, white men. We are not the masters of that social organization and so it towers over us just as Moira, fate, towered over the mythical chauvinist, Oedipus. Women began to fight that corrupting, anti-human, anti-life structure. This beginning is known as the Women's Liberation Movement. However, before there was a WLM there were always a number of women who questioned the system and found it destructive to themselves. Those women became women-identified. I am one of those women. The male culture's word for this kind of woman is Lesbian. This is a narrow definition so typical of the male culture's vulgar conceptual limitations. In their world, the term applies only to sexual activity between women. In our world, to be a *political* Lesbian means to be a woman-identified woman. It means you move toward women and are capable of making a total commitment to women. The male party line concerning Lesbians is that women become Lesbians out of reaction to men. This is a pathetic illustration of the male ego's inflated proportions. I became a Lesbian because of women, because

Woman identified Woman: It means you move toward women and are capable

women are beautiful, strong and compassionate. Secondarily, I became a Lesbian because the culture that I live in is violently anti-woman. How could I, a woman, participate in a culture that denies me my humanity? How can any woman in touch with herself participate in this culture? To give a man support and love before giving it to a sister is to support that culture, that power system, for men receive the benefits of sexism regardless of race or social position. The higher up they are on the color line and the salary line the more benefits they receive, but all men benefit by sexism at some level.

Proof of the pudding is that the most rabid man haters are heterosexual women, and with good reason--they are directly oppressed by individual men. The contradiction of supporting the political system that oppresses you and the individuals who benefit by that system, men, is much more intense for the heterosexual woman than for the homosexual woman. Lesbians are oppressed by the male power system but not by individual men in the same intimate, insidious fashion. Therefore, we Lesbians are the ultimate insult to the sexist male and the world he has built up around his weaknesses. Why? Because we ignore him. Heterosexual women are still caught up in reacting to him. Because we ignore him, because we are the ultimate insult, we pay and we pay heavily. Following are some instances of how a woman pays

# of making total commitment to women.

for Lesbianism in America. The examples are from my direct experience.

In 1962, when I was sixteen, a schoolmate's father threatened to shoot me on sight. He had found love letters that I had written to his daughter. He literally locked the girl up. He drove her to and from school. She couldn't go out at night and she couldn't receive phone calls unless he screened them. He went so far as to go to the administration of the school and have her transferred out of the classes we had together. I also got kicked off student council, thanks to his moral purity. Naturally, our classmates were surprised at my getting bounced and at the sudden ending of my friendship with this girl. Many of them vaguely figured out what was happening. The result of this sleuthing was that our friends split over whether we were Lesbians or whether we weren't. Our closest friends hotly defended us by saying we couldn't possibly be such horrible creatures. Our not-so-close friends smacked their lips over the scandal and in a short time it was all over our high school as well as every other high school in the city. The gossip was shortlived as I flatly stated that I did love the girl and if that was Lesbianism I was glad of it. The gossip stopped and so did the friendships. My closest friends nearly trampled each other in the rush for the door. My civics teacher and student council advisor, a pompous, pasty-faced, balding white man who proudly proclaimed his membership in the John Birch Society, declared as he canned me that I was "unhealthy." I was sick all right but not in the way they imagined--I was sick of all those dirty looks, snickers and outright fights I was having with every loud-mouthed heterosexual who crossed my path.

The next year I went to the state university. I

had won a scholarship which was a good thing because my family's total income for 1962 was $2,300. The university had around 15,000 students, if not from the state itself, from neighboring Southern states. Everything was fine until I became mildly involved in the just beginning civil rights movement. I had been seen on the black side of town. One of my friends called me into her room to talk about my sudden change for the worse. I told her I thought just the opposite about my behavior. She upbraided me for mixing with those people--blacks and Jews (who were behind it all, of course--can you believe it?) I told her I didn't give a rat's ass about race or sex. As far as I was concerned it was the person that counted, not pigment, not sex.

Within three hours of that conversation I was called into the office of the Dean of Women, guardian of morals and the flowers of Southern womanhood. This cheery-faced, apple-cheeked, ex-Marine sergeant offered me a cigarette with a tight-lipped smile and then blasted me with, "Now what's this I hear about your relationships with other women?" She went on to accuse me of seducing the president of Delta Delta Delta, of seducing numerous innocents in the dorms and, sin of sins, of sleeping with black men. She threw in a few black women for good measure. If I had kept such a busy schedule, I think I would have been too exhausted to walk into her office. She hinted in heavy tones that in addition to my numerous sexual perversions I was also a communist and was "stirring up the nigras." In a burst of anger I cracked her with, "How dare you accuse me of Lesbianism when you are a Lesbian yourself? You persecute me to protect yourself, you broad-assed sow." Rational discourse collapsed. She put me under house arrest and I couldn't leave the dorms at night. I was checked hourly by the resident counselor in the dorm and I had the pleasure of reporting to the university psychiatrist once a day and If I didn't the campus guards went out looking for me. My psychiatrist couldn't speak good English but he was a whiz at one English phrase with remarkable enunciation, "You sleep with women?" He had a habit of embracing me after our half hour of international exchange. I question whether those embraces were part of my therapy since he always had a hard on.

All of this happened during exam period. One night I was busy cramming for a physics exam when a self-appointed contingent of physical education majors burst into my room. It was quite a shock since no one had been speaking to me since the beginning of this mess (two weeks' time). They didn't exactly speak to me. Frightened past reason, these wild-eyed women informed me that if I even hinted that they were Lesbians or that any of their beloved faculty fell into that damned category, they would kill me. Nothing like a little melodrama to spice my misery.

The next day, I was treated to a demonstration of how sexism kills what little good there might be left in the human heart. I walked into my exam and silence fell over the crowded auditorium. When I would try to sit in an empty seat, the student next to it would inform me that it was taken, that I should drop dead, that it was broken--plus a few I don't remember. I took my exam sitting on the floor and I know I got an A. I had a 99% average before the exam and the exam itself was easy. When the grades were reported, my average was 61%. No explanation, just 61%.

One final note concerning my university

experience: During my brief encounter with the civil rights movement and the white candy asses who were in it, I found something out that was sure to disquiet the administration of the university. Many of the ramshackle buildings in the black community were owned by city and university officials. The occupants paid double for gas and electricity. Water was drawn from a well. Two or three families were crowded into the building and there were many children. If rent was not paid on time, the landlord's lackeys removed the front door regardless of weather conditions. Most of the people had menial jobs at the university and were paid scratch. A few of us were preparing to write an article on our discovery for the student newspaper. It is more than likely that Lesbianism was the way for the university to throw me out and quash the issue. After all, who is going to listen to a Lesbian?

Southern hospitality does not apply if you are a Lesbian and if you dared to wink an eye at civil rights. I couldn't get a job. My scholarships were suspended so I couldn't go back to school. In other words, I couldn't go home again. I arrived in New York City after a long series of adventures. I felt as though I were in the hanging gardens of neon. Home now was an abandoned red and black Hudson automobile off Washington Square. I lived in the back seat with another orphan--a kitten named Baby Jesus. The front seat was inhabited by Calvin, a South Carolina male homosexual. Calvin had suffered many beatings from his heterosexual black brothers because of his homosexuality. Our pain was a common bond. Nobody wants queers. We stayed together until Calvin found someone to keep him, which didn't take long.

If you are young, female and poor, New York City is worse than Dante's Inferno. You are walking game for all manner of sick hunters. Looking back on those days, I'm not quite sure how I survived. Being a woman-identified woman helped as I was determined not to give in and seek male protection. I got a job as a waitress. I had to wear demeaning clothes, a costume really, and put up with passes that ranged from the tragically transparent to the truly creative. I saved money by living in a cold water flat, without stove and without heat. I had two pair of jeans, two sweatshirts (which I wore inside out as I couldn't bear to see the name of that hated university), and one pair of sneakers. I saved until I could enroll in New York University.

After the first semester I earned a scholarship and in that way I finished my education, an education designed to process you into the white, heterosexual male, middle class world.

During the week I would sometimes go into gay bars. The women I met were interesting. Many were tied into establishment jobs and others were secretaries trying to look like the women tied into the establishment jobs. New York's old gay, lesbian world has as many rules as the tsarina's court. Most often I was struck by the isolation the women enforced upon each other. Oppression runs deep and among our own we sometimes act it out on each other with as much viciousness as the very culture which produced the oppression. It was in gay bars that I learned that a world of women can only work if we destroy the male value system, the male pattern for human relationships (if you can call it human). These methods employ role play, economic exploitation, dominance vs. passivity, and material proof of your social rank. These things can only keep people apart and fighting with each other. As long as you work within that system of values, you can never really know anyone, least of all yourself.

When the rumblings of the just born Women's Liberation Movement reached me, I was filled with hope. I was off to find and join Women's Liberation and to conquer sexism once and for all. What I found was that sexism exists between women in the movement and it is potentially as destructive as the sexism between men and women.

I came to Women's Liberation via a political homosexual group, The Student Homophile League, which three women and about ten men helped to found in 1967 at Columbia University and N.Y.U. I left the homosexual movement because it was male dominated. Homosexual men (with few exceptions) are like heterosexual men in that they don't give a damn about the needs of women. As soon as I heard of it, I went to the National Organization for Women. N.O.W. is not the same as Women's Liberation, but at the time I didn't know that. I went to a few business meetings where the women conducted themselves in a parliamentary manner and played polite power games with each other. There were vague rumors of more radical groups but I couldn't get in touch with any of them. It was almost like prohibition days -- you had to know somebody who knew somebody in those groups. I didn't know anybody, so I gritted my teeth and stuck it out with the golden girls. I sat at the general meetings and said nothing. Eventually a woman did talk to me. I questioned her on the Lesbian issue and she bluntly told me that the word Lesbian was never to be uttered. 'After all, that is exactly what the press wants to say we are, a bunch of Lesbians.' She then went on to patronizingly say, 'What are you doing worrying about Lesbians, you must have a lot of boyfriends.' Okay, sister, have it your way. I kept silent for a few more months. Finally N.O.W. had what it termed a rap session for new women. It was at the apartment of a woman lawyer and was full of stockbrokers, editors, art directors and others of similar professional privilege or aspiring to similar professional privilege. I showed up too, minus the privilege, but I figured that I was a new woman and that's what counts. Anyway, maybe I'd get the chance to open my mouth without standing up and orating about Madam Chairwoman and points of order, etc. The rap session droned on. Women bitched about job discrimination, the pill, etc. Here let me insert a note about my character. I am not a silent, retiring woman. I kept silent up until this meeting, because I was unfamiliar with the organization, because I was born poor and remained poor and I was surrounded by privileged women who took food, housing and education for granted. Lastly, I did not want to jeopardize other Lesbians. By this time I had a few months to review the political issues at stake and to come up with the firm conclusion that N.O.W. was, to make a long story short, full of shit. A women's movement is for women. Its actions and considerations should be for women not for what the white, rich, male heterosexual media finds acceptable. In other words, Lesbianism definitely was an important issue and should be out in the open.

I stood up and said something that went like this: "All I've heard about tonight and in the other meetings is women complaining about men, in one form or other. I want to know why you don't speak about other women? Why you deliberately avoid Lesbianism and why you can't see anything but men? I think Lesbians are ahead of you." (At that time I believed the Lesbian politically superior to the heterosexual woman, and I still do although now I recognize there are such gaps as apolitical Lesbians and political heterosexuals.) What followed my short remarks resembled a mass coronary. One woman jumped up and declared that Lesbians want to be men and that N.O.W. only wants 'real' women. This kind of thing went on for a bit. Then the second wave set in--the sneaky, sly curiosity that culminates in,"Well, what do you do in bed?' (I paint myself green and hang from the rafters.) After approximately one hour of being the group freak and diligently probed, poked and studied, these ladies bountiful decided that, yes, I was human. Yes, I did resemble a young woman in her early twenties. Yes, I even looked like what young women in their early twenties were supposed to look like. (I had long hair and was in a skirt. Now I have short hair and if I wear pants, I'm told I look like a young boy. You figure it out.) There were other Lesbians in the room and they too looked like what women are supposed to look like. The difference between them and me was that I opened my mouth and fought the straight ladies. I was even angrier at my silent sisters than at these incredibly rude, peering, titillated heterosexual wonders. Lesbian silence is nothing new to me, but it never fails to piss me off. I know all the reasons to be quiet in front of the straight enemy, and I find them false. Every time you keep your mouth shut you make life that much harder for every other Lesbian in this country. Our freedom is worth losing your job and your friends. If you keep your mouth shut you are a coward; you silently assert heterosexual imperialism; you allow it to go on by not fighting back. The women in that room were cowards. They thought they could pass for straight. In the last three years since that meeting, every one of them has been brutally purged from N.O.W.-- and they are still silent.

In the room, somehow, a few women got beyond the label, Lesbian, and tried to see me as a person. At the next general meeting, some of them came over and talked to me. They were trying to break down the barriers between us. The N.O.W. leadership was another story. They would in no way recognize the issues of Lesbianism as relevant to the movement. Secretly, a few of them called me and 'confessed' to being Lesbians themselves. They were ashamed of their silences but their logic was, when in Rome do as the Romans do. They were busy playing straight because they didn't want to lose their positions in the leadership. They asked me not to reveal them. There were hints that I could have a place in the leadership if I would play my cards right (shut up). This kind of buy-off is commonly known as being the 'token nigger.' They got a real bargain with me. Not only was I a Lesbian, but I was poor, I was an orphan (adopted) without knowledge of my ethnic origins. At the time, I saw the co-option but I had nowhere else to go and it didn't occur to me then to start a Lesbian movement. I became editor of New York N.O.W.'s newsletter. From that I moved up to being the administrative coordinator for the national organization, an appointed post. It sounds good if you care about titles but what it really means is that you collate, staple, and mail. Everything was fine as long as I did not bring up the Lesbian issue. After all, the issue was solved because I was in the power structure and I was a Lesbian. Being the token Lesbian, I also helped take the heat off the hidden Lesbians. It wasn't right. I knew it wasn't right but I couldn't figure out how to fight it. I still couldn't get in touch with the 'radical' groups and when I mentioned my interest in these groups, a woman on the Executive Board told me they were all a gang of unclean girls who hated Lesbians and who talked about their personal hang-ups. I asked her if she had ever been to a meeting and she said that she hadn't. However, she assured me that she had heard this on very good authority.

As women began to be comfortable with me and see that I was a fairly decent human being, they began to turn on to me. It was very painful for me because when they experienced warm or sexual feelings they began to treat me as a man. All these women knew was men. The old seduction game we learned in pre-school sex-role training-- that's what I was getting. I can't respond to that kind of thing. Some of the women were hurt, some angry and some vicious. Then there was the most manipulative woman of all, the one who was going to liberate herself on my body. She could then pass herself off as a right on brave feminist, because she had slept with a woman. It was pretty confusing. As you can see, the women still thought of Lesbianism as a sexual activity only. This is the way in which men define it. The women couldn't understand that Lesbianism means a different way of living. It means, for me, that you dump all roles as much as possible, that you forget the male power system, and that you give women primacy in your life--emotionally, sexually, personally, politically. It doesn't mean that you look at girlie magazines or pinch the bottoms of passers-by. Difficult as all this was, worse events were to follow. A N.O.W. national officer of much fame made a clumsy pass at me. Not only do I not want to make passes at other women, I don't want women to make passes at me. It all sounds like a football game. Needless to say, I did not respond to the woman.Within an amazingly short time, I was relieved of my duties at the national office for lack of funds. While the leadership was nervously casting its eyes about for someone to take on the burden of the newsletter, I decided to go down fighting. I put out the January 1970 issue of the newsletter with a blast at the leadership for its sexist, racist and class biased attitudes. Two other N.O.W. officers, fed up with the back room politicking and high powered prison guarding, helped with the issue and also publicly resigned their offices.

By this time, I had discovered women of the other groups. I went to Redstockings, an organization which pushed consciousness raising and the pro-woman line. Redstockings was not too pro-woman when it came to Lesbians. They could empathize with the prostitute, support the housewife, encourage the single woman and seek child care for the mother, but they wouldn't touch the Lesbian. The token Lesbian once more, I became more and more depressed. At least, I had enough insight to realize that this was not my personal problem. It was and still is the crucial political issue, the first step toward a coherent, all-woman ideology. But when there is just one person pushing an issue that one person becomes the issue, she becomes a Cassandra of sorts.

Lesbianism is the issue that deals with women reacting positively to other women. All other issues deal with men and the society they have built to contain us. The real question are why are women afraid of one another? Why does the straight woman throttle the Lesbian? Why do women keep insisting this is a bedroom issue and not a political issue, when in fact this issue is at the bottom of our self-image? If we cannot look at another woman and see a human being worth making a total commitment to--politically, emotionally, physically--then where the hell are we? If we can't find another woman worthy of our deepest emotions then can we find ourselves worthy of our own emotion or are all commitments reserved for men, those that benefit by our oppression? It is clear that men are not reserving their deepest commitments for women, otherwise we wouldn't be raped, butchered on abortionists' tables, jeered at in the public streets and denied basic rights under a government that preaches equality. We are taunted in the streets, in the courts, in our homes as though we were nothing more than walking sperm receptacles.

A few Redstocking tried to deal with these issues. They received no support from the other women. By this time I was tired and too wise to spend much energy on the straight ladies. I left the group without recriminations and blow-ups. Those women from the group who have become Lesbians have also left.

The next move was to Gay Liberation, a radical group for homosexuals which began in 1969-70. It supposedly is for men and women. I knew from my previous experience that I wouldn't work with homosexual men again unless something wonderful happened inside their heads and in their system of priorities. But there were gay women there with little women's consciousness and I thought maybe I could push a more feminist understanding among them. It would be a positive step for them as well as me as I needed to be among other Lesbians. Gay Liberation contained women who were highly politicized concerning homosexual oppression so if they could get a consciousness of woman oppression and connect the two, it would be a step forward.

There are good reasons many Lesbians have

no political consciousness of woman oppression. One of the ways in which many Lesbians have protected themselves from the pain of woman oppression is to refuse to see themselves as traditional women. Society encourages this view because if you are not a traditional woman, then you must be some kind of man. This is the other side of the male-identified coin: Heterosexual women live through their men and thereby identify with them, gaining heavy privilege; some Lesbians assume a male role and thereby become male identified, although they receive no political-economic privilege. She wants her own life but the only way to have your own life in this society is to be a man (it also helps to be white and middle class); so many a Lesbian became an imitation man. Other Lesbians feel themselves as women, know intensely that they are not imitation men but stay away from Women's Liberation which could develop their political consciousness. They know from direct experience that straight women cannot be trusted with Lesbian sensibilities and sensitivities. Many of the women in GLF fell into that group. They would rather work with male homosexuals and endure male chauvinism than expose themselves to a more obviously hostile element, the heterosexual woman. More hostile because if her man suspects she is trucking with Lesbians she loses the privileges she gains through association with him. More hostile because Lesbians force her to face herself with no societal props. More hostile because inside she *knows* and she hates herself for her fears.

When I suggested consciousness raising to the women in GLF they were suspicious. They thought I was a Pied Piper wooing them into Women's Liberation instead of fighting homosexual oppression by working through GLF. They didn't bother to ask me much; if they had, they would have found out that I went that route in 1967-68.

In spite of their suspicions, they did form consciousness raising groups. A sense of woman oppression was developed and many were well along the way because of their increasing anger over how the gay men mistreated them. They saw that Lesbian oppression and male homosexual oppression have less in common than they formerly thought. What we have in common is that heterosexuals of both sexes hate and fear us. The similarity stops there because that hate and fear take on vastly different forms for the Lesbian than for the male homosexual. As the months rolled by, a few of the homosexual women began to see that yes, I was human. Yes, I did resemble a young woman in her early twenties, etc. Through the work of those original consciousness raising groups, a new phase was started in the struggle against sexism. Women who love women began to get it together. We are no longer willing to be token Lesbians in the Women's Liberation Front, nor are we willing to be the token women in the Gay Liberation Front.

The first explosion from this new direction came at the Second Congress to Unite Women when the Lesbians (40 in number) confronted the women there. For the first time, straight women were forced to face their own sexism and their complicity with the male power structure.

Since the Congress, in the spring of 1970, Lesbians have come out in ever increasing numbers and the backlash has increased proportionally. Many Lesbians have come to the conclusion that they can no longer work with straight women, women who remain tied to men ideologically as well as individually.

This is a call for a separatist movement of

Lesbians? Yes and No. No, (speaking for myself) because I do not want to be separate from any women. Yes, because until heterosexual women treat Lesbians as full human beings and fight the enormity of male supremacy with us, I have no option but to be separate from them just as they have no option but to be separate from men until men begin to change their own sexism. Separatism is the heterosexual woman's choice by default, not mine.

Separation is what the ruling rich, white male wants: female vs. male; black vs. white; gay vs. straight; poor vs. rich. I don't want to be separate from anyone—that just keeps the Big Man on top of all of us. But I can't work with people who degrade me, don't deal with behavior that is destructive to me and who don't share their privileges. The last thing that I want is separatism. We can only achieve reformist changes for our sub-group if we remain separatists. Together we can change the entire society and make a better life for ourselves individually and collectively.

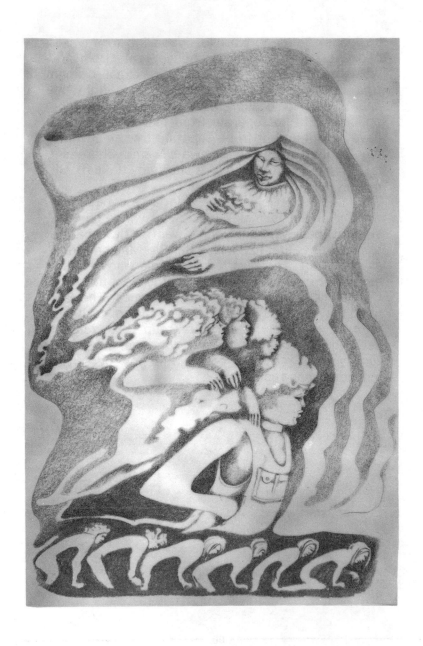

The Last Straw

Now that lesbians are building a separate movement, class is a critical issue among us. Working class lesbians are determined that class will be the first issue resolved within our movement; otherwise the working class lesbians will be unable to work with middle class lesbians. Since class is so misunderstood, since it evokes such wild emotional responses, I will try to explain class in a concrete way, in terms of ideas and behavior. It would be repetitious to explain class in terms of the economy--Marx has already done that for us.

America is a country reluctant to recognize class differences. The American myth crystallized is: This is the land of equal opportunity; work hard, stay in line, you'll get ahead. (Getting ahead always means money.) All public school children are fed this myth. It gives poor people hope and it reinforces middle class people's belief in their own superiority. To prove that this is the land of golden opportunity, elastic capitalism has been able to create enough tokens on many levels to keep the myth alive, i.e., the late Whitney Young, Diana Ross, Margaret Mead, etc. Visually parading the tokens promises working class people, Blacks, Chicanos, and women the chance to get ahead and

Downward mobility is the greatest insult yet devised by middle class people against

channels them into the establishment where they will cut each other's throats to be captialism's newest token. Tokenism also creates a smug security for middle class whites. It allows them to be blind to class differences by showing them the people who have 'made it.' The middle class person then assumes that with extra effort a 'disadvantage' person can get ahead, she just has to work harder. Since middle class people don't socialize or have close job relationships with workers there are no clashing experiences to challenge their false assumptions.

Due to America's peculiar blurring of class distinctions, middle class people do not think in class terms except for those who have become Marxist intellectuals. Middle class people often don't recognize that they are middle class. Even in the various political movements, they may recognize class intellectually but they don't understand how their personal behavior, shot through with middle class assumptions and ideas, is destructive to those of us from the working class. Even those who buy capitalism's line and want to 'make it' know they are 'inferior' due to class background and they work twice as hard to 'overcome' it.

Class is much more than the Left's definition of relationship to the means of production. Class involves your behavior, your basic assumptions about life, your experiences (determined by your

the working class.

class) which validate those assumptions, how you are taught to behave, what you expect from yourself and from others, your concept of a future, how you understand problems and solve them, how you think, feel, act. It is these behavioral patterns cemented in childhood that cause class conflicts in the various movements. It is these behavioral patterns that middle class women resist recognizing although they may be perfectly willing to accept class in Marxist terms, a neat trick that helps them avoid really dealing with class behavior and changing that behavior in themselves. It is these behavioral patterns which must be recognized, understood and changed.

As Lesbians it is crucial that we make these changes immediately. We have few privileges in male society if we come out because we threaten male supremacy at its core. Does that mean that because we have few class/race privileges in male society that we have a no class/race differences among ourselves? No. While lesbians have little power to enforce their privileges once they *come out* they still continue to behave in the ways of their class/race. It is that behavior which infuriates those of us who are not middle class and who are not white. Our anger confuses the white, middle class lesbian because she can't understand what she is doing wrong--her behavior seems natural to her.

As examples, I have singled out two ideas and their consequent behavior current in the Lesbian Movement which are harmful to working class lesbians. All too often these mistakes are deliberate stalls on the part of the middle class lesbians to keep from changing themselves. Rather than hear us, they resist us with accusations and theories to negate our demand that they change oppressive behavior.

I. The Idea that a Working Class Woman with a College Education Escapes her Class Background

Middle class women theorize that if you are working class but have a college degree then you must have just as much class privilege as they do so you are no longer working class. This idea is sheer arrogant blindness. Just because many of us fought our way out of inadequate schools into the universities and became "educated" in no way removes the entire experience of our childhood and youth--working class life. A degree does not erase all that went before it. A degree simply means that you have submitted to white, male, heterosexual, middle class educational standards and passed. It doesn't mean you accept those standards. If you have a college degree you can get a better job than if you don't have one. (Unless you are a lesbian who has come out.) None of us working class women are trying to pretend we can't get better jobs with degrees than without degrees...but a job is a way to earn money in adulthood, our pasts remain the same and our ways can remain intact.

A white, middle class woman wouldn't dream of telling a Black lesbian with a college degree that she is no longer Black, yet she feels perfectly justified in telling a working class woman with a degree that she is no longer working class! There is a reason for this double think. Working class lesbians with degrees push middle class lesbians very hard. We aren't intimidated by their high tone raps and we can talk "their" language only with "our" ideas. This scares the shit out of them, many of them want to believe the class stereotype: working class people are inarticulate, shy, passive, uninterested in ideas, etc. Those of us who fight back destroy those illusions and we also destroy the middle class person's class power by doing so. The women who are the most hostile to "educated" working class women are very often, middle class women who want to cling to class behavior and the power it gives them over other women. The other middle class women usually aren't hostile, just conveniently confused, so confused that it takes them a good long time before they believe us and change their own behavior. And disbelief of a working class woman's analysis of her class oppression is one more way to undermine us-- we don't "know enough" to analyze our own goddamn oppresion, we need a middle class woman to do it for us in fancy sociological language. Christ.

College was culture shock to many of us from the working class. College is middle class and reinforces the white middle class woman in her class ways. College for the working class woman challenges her entire life experience. The snobbism rampant in humanities departments, the enforced practice of saying in three polysyllabic paragraphs what could be said in two short sentences are counter to working class ways. There are literally hundreds of slaps in the face that a working class woman endures. Middle class women endure the sexism of college but not the classism. Working class women get both, Third World women get it three ways. For us, college was a journey through a hostile environment, an environment where we were forced to deny our class background in order to get our degree.

College caused some working class women to reject their early lives, adopt middle class values, become upwardly mobile (or if they joined a political movement, downwardly mobile) and fight their own working class sisters to be accepted into the middle class world. Others of us endured college because we didn't want to repeat the lives of drudgery and misery our parents had, but we did not adopt middle class ways. For many of us college was the last straw that pushed us into open class resistance.

Perhaps the most outrageous aspect of the middle class women's views on education and working class women is their unspoken assumption that we went to college because we were upwardly mobile--in other words, we wanted to be like them. Only a woman far removed from bread and butter reality could harbor such an assumption. We watched our parents slave for nothing. School seemed the answer to our economic plight if we could just get there. So we studied, got scholarships, took out loans that kept us in hock for years--to avoid that same futile labor of our parents, to survive economically rather than subsist. And in this pursuit working class women suffered more than working class men because of sex discrimination in admission and scholarships. (Plus you had to hide being lesbian or you'd get thrown out.) In spite of all these difficulties, this generation of working class lesbians and women from twenty-two to thirty-five has many college graduates, a testament of grit if ever there was one. For many of us school was the first opportunity we had to have *time* to think politically. When you work all day, every day, there is little time to think and no time to politically organize. Yes we have college degrees, no we don't work in factories like our parents did and we learned from the rape of our parents--we want to make a revolution because of it.

II. Downward Mobility as the Road to Removing Class Differences

Youth/drug culture, the New Left, the Women's Movement and unfortunately, the Lesbian Movement are all choking on this idea. Downward mobility is a mockery of working class life. It is poverty made fashionable. Behavior remains the same: Those who don't comply with this "hip" lifestyle are looked down upon. It is in the establishment of hierarchies that the middle class betrays itself--they always have to look down on somebody, an habitual attitude of power.

I don't want to live with mattresses on the floor, ragged clothes, dirt and spaghetti for supper every night. How anyone can imitate poverty and give it the flavor of "inness" is so alien to me that it is disgusting. I don't want to be above anybody but I do want decent housing, nice clothes and good food.

Downward mobility is the greatest insult yet devised by middle class people against the working class. If that alone isn't enough, downward mobility is married to the mistrust of the mind and a worship of the emotional. First of all, I don't understand intellect/emotional divisions yet millions of people seemed chained to that separation. A woman who thinks and analyzes is accused of being a power-hungry 'heavy' in the movement while a woman who cries at every meeting is embraced as a true sister. Many middle class women, fearing that intellect will be mistaken for middle class behavior and remembering *their* college experience, bury their brains in a morass of "vibes," "gut feelings," and outright hysteria. This is dogmatically declared "true woman" behavior since men don't express their feelings. Serious organizing to end our oppression is suspect, ideological struggle is heresy; feelings are the way, the light and the truth--even when they result in political stagnation. Such an idea spells death to real political change if people cling to it.

It isn't intellect that working class women mistrust in middle class women, it is how middle class women use their intellect to rationalize holding onto class behavior that hurts us. Or simply, we mistrust bullshit, not brains.

Difficult as it is for middle class women to realize how downward mobility strikes us, they must open themselves and see what they are doing to us. I know that for many middle class women, downward mobility was a first attempt at trying to change their ways. However, those women must realize that the irony of downward mobility, its fatal flaw, is that they could *afford* to become downwardly mobile. Their class privilege enabled them to reject materialism. For those of us who grew up without material advantages downward mobility is infuriating--here are women rejecting what we never had and can't get! Valid as that emotional reaction is on our part, we working class women are being taught a lesson by the middle class women. That lesson is: lots of capitalistic possessions and social status do not bring happiness--another American myth shattered.

One good idea behind downward mobility is non-consumerism. The problem is not the idea but how it has become part of a new middle class "hip" lifestyle, an inverse snobbism that hits working class people both ways: Before downward mobility we were invisible or when visible, we were trash; with downward mobility we are "counter-revolutionaries" because we don't comply with the "hip" lifestyle. It's the same old shit--middle class people develop their values and measure us by their standards and have the effrontery to be enraged if we measure them by *our* standards. Downward mobility is the other side of the capitalistic coin, or to put it more bluntly, the East Village is second generation Scarsdale.

Political working class lesbians are obviously going to practice non-consumerism but we aren't creating a behavioral code out of it. We aren't trucking around in patched pants mumbling about "gettin in touch with our feelins." (Another downward mobility insult, middle class women parody our speech to prove how they are no longer middle class. This is as unforgiveable as a white person putting on a broad Black "accent.")

Downward mobility also has one other dangerous effect upon those of us from the working classes--it prevents us from benefiting from the material privileges of white, middle class women. If you have money, sister, don't deny it, *share* it. If you have advanced skills, don't make pottery in your loft, teach us those skills. If you have good clothes, don't walk around in rags, give us some of your clothes. Downward mobility is a way to deny your material privileges to prove how "right on" you are. We know that anytime you get tired of poverty you can go right back to them (unless, of course, you have publicly come out).

Downward mobility assumes that material benefits are bad. That's a mistake. Material benefits aren't bad, what's bad is that everyone doesn't have them. Downward mobility insures that working class women still won't have material benefits--we have more trouble getting them than the middle class woman and she won't share her privileges with us, she's too busy living in a dump. *Share* your material benefits.

Downward mobility and ideas centering around education are just two examples of how class can shatter alliances, make people hate each other, weaken us politically. Those examples are critical of middle class women and they deserve criticism but I'm not saying that middle class women are inevitably horrible. All I'm saying is that they have to change those ways. I am also not saying that being working class is wonderful and makes you an instant lesbian revolutionary. The fact is that there are class/race differences between lesbians and those differences have to be wiped out because they keep us apart and keep us at each other's throats. Behavior born of privilege granted from white, upper class, male heterosexuals is destructive to women and must be ended. The more privileged you were in that old world, the more you must work to free yourself from that destructiveness so that you can build the new world. But we have all lived in Amerika and in some ways we all have to change.

In the past those of us from working class backgrounds tried to make this clear to straight sisters. We are now making it crystal clear to our middle class lesbian sisters. It is not our job to explain our oppression to you, you must work to find out how class hurts other women. Don't waste our time by trying to prove you are an exception because your father was working class and your mother was middle class. All that means is that you have a mixture of class ways; stop trying to wriggle out of those middle class ways that you *do* have. Change them. You are your own responsibility. It is your job to examine yourself and change just as it is my job to examine myself and change. Our collective responsibility as lesbians is to annihilate, smash, destroy male supremacy and build a New World.

The real question is not whether you are middle class and white but whether you are serious about destroying male supremacy, about changing the world. If you are serious you will begin by changing yourself.

The Shape of
Things to Come

If you love women then you are in revolt
against male supremacy. The world which men
have built hates women. Women, according to male
supremacy, exist to serve the male. A woman who
loves women then defies the basic building block of
male supremacy: woman hatred. Women who love
women are Lesbians. Men, because they can only
think of women in sexual terms, define Lesbian as
sex between women. However, Lesbians know that
it is far more than that, It is a different way of life. It
is a life determined by a woman for her own benefit
and the benefit of other women. It is a life that
draws strength, support and direction from women.
About two years ago this concept was given the
name woman-identified woman. That's not a bad
name, it is just a fancy way of saying that you love
yourself and other women. You refuse to limit
yourself to the male definitions of women. You free
yourself from male concepts of "feminine"
behavior.

Lesbianism, politically organized, is the
greatest threat that exists to male supremacy. How
can men remain supreme, how can they oppress
women if women reject them and fight the entire
world men have built to contain us? The beginning

The embryo of this concept, of organized struggle, is slowly growing.

rejection is to put women first in your life, put yourself first. If you do that then you begin to understand that the only way you can lead the life you would like to lead is by smashing male supremacy--and its offshoot oppressions, class and race supremacy.

Any oppressed person who gives in to her oppression insures that others will remain oppressed and she exposes her sisters who are fighting that oppression. The emerging political Lesbians, or women-identified women, realize the scope of male supremacy and are changing their lives to fight it. Women who remain silent leave these outspoken women to face the common oppressor. Committing yourself to women is the first concrete step toward ending that common oppression. If you cannot find it in yourself to love another woman, and that includes physical love, then how can you truly say you care about women's liberation? If you don't feel other women are worthy of your total commitment--love, energy, sex, all of it--then aren't you really saying that women aren't worth fighting for? If you reserve those "special" commitments for men then you are telling other women they aren't worth those commitments, they aren't important. You also don't understand or else avoid recognizing that an individual relationship-- your "personal" life--is political. Relationships between men and women involve power, dominance, role play and oppression. A man has the entire system of male privilege to back him up. Another woman has nothing but her own self. Which relationship is better for you? It's obvious.

If women still give primary commitment and energy to the oppressors how can we build a strong movement to free ourselves? Did the Chinese love and support the capitalists? Do the Viet Cong cook supper for the Yankee? Are Blacks supposed to disperse their communities and each live in a white home? The answer, again, is obvious. Only if women give their time to women, to a women's movement, will they be free. You do not free yourself by polishing your chains, yet that is what heterosexual women do.

Lesbians who have tried to pull women into a supportive women's community are often attacked by these heterosexual women who hang onto the privileges they get from their men. These Lesbian-haters are not always vicious women. Most of them don't understand because If they did then they would have to change their lives and lose the scant privileges men have given them. The facts are simple: Heterosexuality keeps women separated from each other. Heterosexuality ties each woman to a man. Heterosexuality exhausts women because they struggle with their man--to get him to stop oppressing them--leaving them little energy for anything else. For this destruction of women's communities, for this betrayal of other women, women indeed get privileges from men: legitimacy (you are a real woman If you are with a man--a sexual definition again), prestige, money, social acceptance, and in some token cases political acceptance.

If you are a Lesbian who has come out then you cut yourself off from those privileges. You have ended your stake in maintaining the heterosexual world. You are in total revolt against male supremacy. How can women liberate themselves if they are still tied to that male supremacist world? How can a woman tied to men through hetero-sexuality keep from betraying her sisters? When push comes to shove, she will choose her man over other women; heterosexuality demands that she make that choice. How can you build a serious political movement when women do this to each other? You can't. Lesbianism is a necessary step in the struggle for liberation.

Why would any heterosexual woman give up the privileges men grant her for being heterosexual? Most often she will only give them up if she sees there is something better than the crumbs thrown to her from men. What can Lesbianism offer? It offers double oppression. It offers the threat of getting fired from your job, estranged from your family and old straight friends, it offers getting your throat slit by straight women in the service of men, it offers constant struggle against an inhumane and diseased world where violence is the key to power and love is a word found in poetry but not on the streets. Why take on those burdens?

Because Lesbianism also offers you the freedom to be yourself. It offers you potential equal relationships with your sisters. It offers escape from the silly, stupid, harmful games that men and women play, having the nerve to call them "relationships." It offers change. You will change yourself by discovering your woman-identified self, by discovering other women. No one, not even another Lesbian, can tell you who that self is. It is your individual challenge, your life. You will be on unfamiliar ground with no old patterns to guide you. As you change yourself you will begin to change your society also. A free, strong self cannot live in the muck that men have made. You will make mistakes and suffer from them. You will hurt and be hurt trying to find new ways. But you will learn and push on. You will discover the thousand subtle ways that heterosexuality destroyed your true power; you will discover how male supremacy destroys all women and eventually the creators of it, men. You will find once your consciousness is raised it cannot be unraised. Once you have a vision of the new world you can no longer accept the old one. You will become a fighter. You will find love and that you are beautiful, strong and that you care. You will build communities with other women from all classes and races, those communities will change the material parts of our lives. You will share what you have with others and they with you. You will revolt against this whole filthy world that tried to cover you and your beauty under a ton of male supremacist slime. That is what Lesbianism offers you.

Those of us who have found those new lives, that hope and courage, find ourselves in the position of being attacked and undermined by women in the women's liberation movement to say nothing of forces outside that movement. We cannot allow ourselves to be oppressed by men; how then can we turn around and allow ourselves to be oppressed and harassed by women clinging to heterosexual privilege? We can't. Therefore, large portions of the political Lesbian population in women's liberation and gay liberation have split from those movements in order to survive. Does that mean we hate straight women? No. But would you volunteer your neck for someone to step on? Does this mean we can never again work with straight women or with gay men? No. But we aren't going to work with anyone until they begin to change their behavior. Some changes are they can no longer push us around, hide us under rugs or try to seduce us when everyone else has gone home only to deny us in the morning.

Straight women by virtue of being tied to men don't understand Lesbians or the political meaning of Lesbianism. Straight women don't know what our lives are like. They can't think like we do. We understand their lives because we were all raised to be straight. It is one-way communication. Straight women are confused by men, don't put women first. They betray Lesbians and in its deepest form, they betray their own selves. You can't build a strong movement if your sisters are out there fucking with the oppressor.

Further, as long as men have women under their control, they aren't going to change. By withdrawing support, men have to change. Sure a few individual men here and there will and have changed. Those few treat you and other women like human beings, but those men still haven't joined in the organized battle against sexism. They have to throw in their lot with us like any group dedicated to political change. Straight women are constantly bought off by the good behavior of a few rare men. Good behavior is not enough, he must join the struggle and take risks like the rest of us. Until that time, no man is our brother, he is still our oppressor. We can't work with straight women while they are misled by "good" men.

A short note about bisexuality. You can't have your cake and eat it too. You can't be tied to male privileges with the right hand while clutching to your sister with the left. Lesbianism is the only road toward removing yourself from male ways and toward beginning to learn equality.

Equality teaches strong lessons. Once you feel your strength you cannot bear the thought of anyone else being beaten down. All other oppressions constructed by men become horrible to you, if they aren't already. Class and race, those later-day diseases, have sprung from sexism itself. No oppression is tolerable. All must be destroyed. Once you have come out you can no longer fall back on race and class privilege, if you have any. Those privileges divide you from your Lesbian sisters who don't have them. Any Lesbian who tries to salvage her racial and class privileges does so at the expense of other Lesbians; she weakens all of us by this mistake. A mistake in recognizing the hatred of male supremacy for Lesbians, also; men award privilege for serving them—the Lesbian does not serve them, so you will be clinging to your privilege without really having the power to back it up. All you have left is the behavioral patterns born of those privileges, the bark without the bite—but that bark turns away other Lesbians. You don't automatically stop acting in those ways. In most cases you have to be taught by your Lesbian sisters who lacked those privileges and understand how divisive they are.

None of this is easy. Becoming a Lesbian does not make you instantly pure, perpetually happy and devotedly revolutionary. But once you have taken your life in your hands you will find you are no longer alone. There is a growing movement of Lesbians dedicated to our freedom, to your freedom, to ending all man-made oppressions. You will be part of that surge forward and you will leave your fingerprints on the shape of things to come.

The following is a very brief outline of practical programs which is the first step toward organized struggle:

I. *Work Projects:* Women with economic privilege, whether straight or Lesbian, Black, Asian, Indian, Latin or White, should organize to meet the survival needs of women without economic privilege. This means food distribution centers, child care centers, health care centers, self-defense programs, skills centers and halfway houses.

II. *Consciousness Raising:* For all its abuses

and misuse, consciousness raising still remains a good step toward understanding one's own oppression. If the C-R is disciplined, each woman should learn from other women and her own life how those lives are a response to the dominant culture, the existing power structure. Women should learn that their personal lives reflect power politics on an individual level. By examining those lives and then going further to connect those lives into a pattern, women learn the mechanics of oppression. Once you know how something works you can fix it or fight it.

III. *Media:* We must develop and extend our own media--newspapers, films, magazines, art, music, etc. The existing white, male, rich media institutions distort the truth of any political movement and get rich off reporting our oppression in the bargain (i.e., David Susskind). It is imperative that we build our own media. No serious political movement in history has ever relied on the communications of its oppressor. Without our own media we are without voice.

IV. *Ideology:* Before we can advance as a political force, we must have a coherent, comprehensive ideology--a body of ideas that analyze our oppression in all its ramifications, economic, political, social, etc. A body of ideas that constructs the way to end that oppression. Lesbianism is the cornerstone for this structure. It is the touchstone of our independence, self-image, creativity. It is the distillation of women's oppression and the crystallization of women's power. Without this as our intellectual base we are doomed to reformism and disunity.

V. *Organization:* These last few years have seen work projects, C-R, the beginnings of media and the beginnings of clear ideology, spring up throughout the country. All these activities are progressing at different rates of speed, different levels of understanding. If we are to forge a powerful political instrument to end our oppression then these activities must be coordinated toward that common purpose. This means that we must be organized, we must be a party. We must concentrate our forces rather than scatter them. The embryo of this concept of organized struggle is slowly growing. Lesbians are realizing that there will be no real political change without a party. Within five years we will have our party. With the formation of that body we will begin the second phase of our struggle against over 10,000 years of servitude. Forward, sisters, forward.

Roxanne Dunbar

The following article is a comment on Roxanne Dunbar's latest work, "The Movement and the Working Class."

I hesitate to write this response to Roxanne Dunbar's latest article because it is so critical. There are women and men who will lick their lips at the prospect of one woman raised in the working class criticizing another. Therefore, let me state that this article is a political criticism, not a personal attack. Criticism is a form of respect because you take the individual seriously enough to reply to her ideas.

"The Movement and the Working Class" is both helpful and harmful. It takes a sharp look at the various groups existent in the U.S. The article does us all a service by analyzing how the different movements ignore class or sell working class people down the river. It is unfair to summarize the article, you owe it to yourself to read it. The point here is to single out areas where Roxanne Dunbar had overlooked something or made a disastrous mistake.

The most glaring factual error in the article is that the author includes the Lesbian movement under the banner of the New Left and then goes on

As long as women. . .cushion reality for them, serve them, men aren't going to change.

to vilify that struggle as being totally removed from the class struggle. She represents Lesbians as promoting bourgeois ideology. Nothing could be further from fact.

"The young people who make up the base of the New Left are organized by 'constituencies.' There is 'Gay Liberation' and 'Women's Liberation' which have merged at points into a more virulent, all-female form called 'Radical Lesbians.'" In this quote from her article, Roxanne simply puts us all in the same pot and throws it out the window. There is no explanation, just a slam in the word "virulent." The fact is that the Lesbian struggle has been operating in this country since the '50's when a group of lesbians formed Daughters of Bilitis. The majority of those women were not working class but they did pull themselves together at a dangerous time--in the middle of the McCarthy era when homosexuality was as great a sin as communism. The Lesbian movement is older than the New Left and has little to do with fashionable radicalism among white, middle class youth.

A second push toward Lesbian organizing came through oppression suffered by young Lesbians from all classes in the Women's Liberation Movement and the Gay Liberation Movement--the push was to get out of the boat. Some of these women, particularly the ones of middle class origin, are more tainted with youth culture rhetoric than the older DOB women or the Lesbians who came out on their own, independent of political movements.

Roxanne is one of the women who turned Lesbians away from the Women's Liberation Movement by her insistence that Lesbianism was a bedroom issue. This is a variation of the same argument that men use against women when women fight for their own liberation. It's the old "your oppression isn't all that important" line. As men deal with women only as sexual beings so Roxanne locks Lesbians in the bedroom.

Roxanne goes on to put us down by saying, "--nothing could be further removed from the class struggle than the question of homosexuality as a freedom, even among homosexuals in the working class. Nothing could be further removed from the consciousness of a working woman with children than the 'freedom' to be a Lesbian." As a woman born and raised in the working class who is a Lesbian living with other working class Lesbians (and some from the middle class) I know this is not true. Except for two of us, all the working class women are new Lesbians and since becoming Lesbians have doubled their work output; they are also happier. They are free from having their energies drained by struggles with individual men or with men in groups. Now they pool their energies with other women and have that much more time for political work. Materially we have pooled our resources and don't have to spend as much time working outside at straight jobs. When is it counter to class struggle to free people more to work in the fight to end class oppression, race oppression, sex oppression?

Roxanne attempts to smash Lesbianism by treating it as a personal luxury rather than dealing with it as a political ideology. This sweeping us under the rug as some great apolitical, individual-istic freedom is classic heterosexual blindness. Her thesis that Lesbianism is a simple personal choice is a cover to avoid recognizing the political implication of Lesbianism: Lesbianism is the greatest threat to male supremacy that exists. As for this simple choice, this unimportant freedom--which frees women's bodies, heads, time and energies—it is

also the freedom to get fired from jobs, betrayed by **straight** women in the movement and spit at by **one's** own race and class. Why? Because if all women were Lesbians male supremacy would have the impossible task of maintaining itself in a vacuum. Men know what a threat we are to their power so they heap the worst abuse upon the Lesbian in order to keep women from becoming Lesbians. They also know that when their male supremacist order topples so will race and class differences since it is not in our self interest to foster divisions based on race and class. Male supremacists foster those divisions, especially the white, rich variety, because it keeps people fragmented and preserves their power. If people are divided from one another they will not unite against the common oppressor, the white, rich capitalist male. This ruling class male encourages working class men of all races to participate in his system by giving those men the power of sexism. Depending on their usefulness to his plans he can also bestow race and class privilege on men. In this way he can turn those men against other men below them who see the truth and organize to end the white, rich man's rule. He can also turn all men, not just segments of the male population, against all women who would organize to end sexist oppression--the privilege all men share: They control the women in their subgroup. The big man preys on the other men's fears of losing control over their women to keep them from seeing that attack on him, The Big Man, weakens his power. So by oppressing women, particularly Lesbians since they fight sexism the hardest, working class males are cutting their own throats. The Big Man controls their jobs, housing and worse, the inside of their heads for he has shaped their concept of masculinity, he has forced them to identify with him both emotionally and economically. Even the man farthest away from The Big Man, the working class Black male, identifies with The Man's phallic imperialism. Roxanne Dunbar's smothering of the politics of working class Lesbians keeps all men, especially working class men, from understanding how sexism most benefits the ruling class male. It keeps the working class man from changing those parts of his behavior that oppress Lesbians and women. No solid alliance can be built between working class women and men until he changes his oppressive actions toward women. The only people who effectively challenge those oppressive actions are Lesbians, and Roxanne, a woman, legitimizes male power by writing off Lesbians. So once again we have political struggle in the hands of men. This time it is the class struggle with a few token women to mask male oppressiveness.

Does this mean that working class Lesbians are intent upon destroying working class men and weakening the class struggle? No, it does not. It means that working class Lesbians are not going to work for an ideology, practical plan or people who oppress us. Men have not purged themselves of supremacist behavior regardless of class/race background. To encourage women to ally with them now perpetuates our oppression. How will men, especially working class men, learn to shed sexism? If we leave them flat, that's how. As long as there is a woman to wipe their noses, cushion reality for them, serve them, men aren't going to change. When women remove themselves from the dominion of men, the men will have a hard time hanging onto sexist behavior and ideas. The male concept of self depends on the subservience and debasement of women. Male power depends on female acceptance of it. If you don't accept their power then they don't have any. Only the rich, white capitalist will have power and that will be economic--and that too, can be crushed.

Also, when we are gone who will be men's escape valves, shit-workers, peacemakers? Without our necks to stand on for a better view the men will be forced to look at themselves and change. The serious ones will join women in the struggle against this society/state international sore.

This same process holds for straight women. As long as they do male supremacy's dirty work and keep Lesbians down, Lesbians must leave the straight women to wallow in a cesspool of their own making. Sexism is not limited to men and must be fought wherever it is found.

By keeping straight women from seeing that Lesbianism is political, that their individual lives and the relationships in it are political, Roxanne allows straight women to continue to support individual men as well as collective male supremacy. The political Lesbian is committed to the destruction of male supremacy, therefore the Lesbian is serious about a women's movement.

Roxanne gives straight women an excuse for not building a strong women's movement to destroy male supremacy. You can't build a women's movement if women are tied to their oppressors-- individually and ideologically. Holding onto male values and privileges granted to women for hetero-sexuality (which insures that each man will have his slave) subverts the women's movement. You cannot build a women's movement if you don't commit yourselves to women, totally. Heterosexual women are still committed to men. Roxanne guarantees that they will stay that way.

Lesbians contain the only hope for women to

realize their own strength, their political power. This explains why working class Lesbians prefer to work with Lesbians in the Lesbian movement (a mixed class movement to smash male supremacy) rather than work with heterosexual working class women in a movement devoted solely to class oppression. Why work with someone who ties you to your oppressor when you have just freed yourself from him on a one-to-one level? Why work in a movement that drains your energies fighting the supremacist attitudes of your supposed working class brothers--who will also try to screw you? Why work with someone who derides your oppression or who actively supresses you with another brand of Marxist intellectualism?

We'll be damned if we'll work with people who oppress us, no matter what class they come from. Roxanne herself says, "for the working class and the poor, the loss of one of its number from the struggle is a great loss--." Yet she insists on insuring that working class Lesbians defect from her appointed class struggle.

By cutting down Lesbians without ever dealing with our politics, by lumping us with the New Left and middle class concerns, Roxanne safely avoids the real crises that would be caused by a meeting of working class women and men. The crisis being that the men would be forced to stop oppressing the women and both would be forced to stop oppressing the Lesbian.

Like many women faced with the choice of renouncing their heterosexual privilege and fighting sexism/racism/classism, Roxanne has chosen to retreat into class struggle, heterosexual to the core. This pattern is repeated wherever Lesbians have asserted themselves. To become a Lesbian is to renounce all sexist privileges,

privileges which keep you apart from other women. Men refuse to give privileges to women who reject their control. Lesbians reject male control and lose heterosexual securities. But they gain through that loss--women.

By turning your back on sexist struggle and embracing class as the only road to liberation, straight women allow men to retain their power over women. They also have the added advantage of being taken seriously as class struggle has a respectable history--after all, it includes men. The battle against sexism is, to date, exclusively a women's fight.

You get points from men for joining a heterosexual class struggle and you get bonus points for attacking Lesbians who are the people attacking sexism. Once again, men have gotten women to do their dirty work for them. Having the straight women attack the Lesbians, their hands remain clean.

Another debilitating feature of the class struggle as it now exists is that it allows middle class people to "join" it. These people reared in middle class homes do not have to give up their privileges or their behavioral patterns cemented in childhood, patterns that are destructive to people reared in working class homes. Often these middle class joiners do not even have to share their material resources with the working class people. All too often all they have to do is accept the intellectual premises of class struggle and go on to organize others for the fight. How revolutionary.

The world has witnessed a number of class revolutions led by Marxist intellectuals who originated in the middle class. In all those countries women still do not share political power commensurate with their number. Their economic situation is improved but that hardly alters the realities of political power: Women have none. In Cuba for all its miracles, sexism is so fierce that homosexuals are "rehabilitated." To tell a woman, especially a working class Lesbian, to repeat the class struggle as defined by men in this country, is to tell her to forget her own oppression, tow the class line, to once more, like a good woman, give herself over to politics as constructed by men.

Sexism is rampant under socialism. Having seen what happens to women repeatedly in class revolutions it is clear that we must try another way.

Does this mean we junk class struggle? As a person who grew up in the working classes I can hardly endorse that. I believe the class and race struggle is and must be part of the fight against sexism. This is an absolute truth for Lesbians. It is not in our self-interest to promote oppression based on class and race. We are despised by all sects, to continue among ourselves destructive divisions of class/race invented by rich, white capitalist men is to commit political suicide. A Lesbian who comes out loses many of her class/race privileges although she doesn't necessarily lose her behavioral patterns that reek of those disgusting privileges. No one wants their Lesbians--not the rich, not the poor, not the Black, not the White, not Roxanne Dunbar. We need each other. We cannot weaken ourselves by hurting each other with left-over daggers from white, rich, capitalist male America. Lesbians, of all people, have the greatest stake in destroying class and racial oppression.

You can't destroy class without destroying capitalism. A Lesbian movement is necessarily socialist. A socialist movement is not necessarily non-sexist. Therein lies the great gap between Roxanne Dunbar and myself.

Roxanne missed this precisely because she is not a Lesbian. No straight woman knows what a Lesbian's life is like and she never will as long as she remains straight. She has not suffered the ultimate sexist oppression. The Lesbian has. She has not experienced Lesbian strength/love. The Lesbian has. Roxanne thinks that Lesbian communities are a New Left hoax. We know they are a tiny space of freedom we have created in the male world. We know they are the beginning of the end for male supremacy and its hideous younger brothers, racial oppression and class oppression.

A word of common sense. When I speak of Lesbians and Lesbian communities, I am not speaking about all Lesbians everywhere. I am speaking about those women who have developed a political ideology, who have committed themselves to the destruction of male supremacy, et. al., who have committed themselves to women, who want to build a new world. I know full well there are women who physically love other women who could sell us out as quickly as any man or straight woman. Some of them are racist, class snobs and outright reactionaries. By the same token, all working class people are not committed to the destruction of capitalism. There are plenty of racists and fascists among the workers. The essential point is that workers carry the greatest threat to capitalism if organized just as Lesbians carry the greatest threat to male supremacy if organized.

Roxanne envisions organizing by breaking through the brainwash of ruling class ideology in the workers. She is absolutely right. But she had better break through the brainwash of male supremacist ideology in her own head or she and other women like her will find themselves deeply betrayed by their own analysis.

Gossip

Gossip is irresponsible communication. Irresponsible because it is at the expense of another person who is not there to defend herself. Irresponsible because it is not constructive: it helps no one, least of all the person being gossiped about. We have all experienced being gossiped about so we know the end result: it destroys trust. It's bad enough when this activity flares up among friends, but when it crops up in a political movement it jeopardizes our security and detracts from political issues.

Women gossip because we will be listened to by other women; gossip is often the only way women can get an audience. With some exceptions, women are excluded from TV and radio broadcasting and newspaper reporting and editorializing. Men have determined that women have nothing to say, and women have internalized their own "unimportance" and term their speaking and listening to other women "gossip."

Given our rigid roles as sex object, mother and maid, it is surprising that over the centuries women did not lose the power of speech altogether. We spoke to each other about those areas of life left to us: child care, domestic chores, maintaining our

Gossip is irresponsible communication.

status as desirable sex objects, and each other. In talking about each other we glossed over the good things and seized upon the bad. Women are ready, so ready to listen and accept negative information about each other. This upsetting activity stems directly from our oppression and subsequent self-hatred. Most women's lives still are a tedium of muffled unhappiness. Aside from TV, one of the few escape routes left is getting involved in other people's lives vicariously. Gossip aides this escape.

How reassuring to hear that Mary is as wretched as you are, or better yet, worse off. That means Mary is "less" than you are and therefore you can feel superior. Given our low status in the pecking order it is a very real consolation to be able to peck someone beneath us. And who is lower than a woman except another woman who has transgressed in her assigned womanly duties or who has freaked out because she could no longer bear her oppression? You also get status if you are the first to know something about another person and you can feel superior.

Gossip is especially destructive when it is aimed at women who are political, and when its content, although appearing to be "personal," is a thinly veiled attack on the victim's politics. There are many types of gossip; this article will discuss two of the most dangerous kinds. First, an example of the "emotional appeal" method.

Mary has formed a political study group with other women. The emotional appeal gossip would say something like this to an unwary listener: "I'm so upset and feel so rejected. Mary, Jane, Susan and Evelyn have formed a study group and left me out. Mary and I used to be good friends. How could she do something like this to me?" What the speaker has failed to tell the listener is exactly that--why she is not part of that group. The speaker has put the formation of a political study group on emotional terms, centered it around herself and her supposed needs. She gives no hint at what the political differences between herself and the group are. The speaker has created an aura of pity for herself. Women are suckers for this kind of emotional appeal because emotions are our assigned sphere by men. This form of gossip is especially disgusting because it preys on women's emotional susceptibility which comes from woman oppression.

The second and more destructive type of gossip is the pseudo-psychological method which includes emotional elements to bolster its claims of the listener's attention. It is connected with class privilege whereas the emotional appeal is not. You have to have had some contact with middle class psychological bullshit in order to be able to pull off this technique--obviously, well-educated middle class women are standouts in its performance.

This form of gossip is vicious and the hardest to track down because it offers some kind of explanation for another woman's behavior that is easy to swallow, and once digested, the listener can turn around and pass it on as her own idea. With emotional appeal alone, the listener can only relate how the poor gossip has been injured by Mary. Here's a brief example of this method--it is best performed over a few weeks or months time so the gossip can build up credibility with the listener and round out her thesis.

"I've known Mary for some time now and we used to be very close. She is a very ambitious and insecure woman. She has to prove herself better than anyone else and she really needs to control people because that is the only way she can be sure about them. Now she has gone and organized this study group with her lackeys and it's only to dominate others that she's doing this. You really should stay away from her, and don't try to work with that study group.'' Again, gossip ignores the political basis of the study group and chooses to single out Mary, whom she dislikes, in order to turn people against Mary and the group. Most political statements or ideas can be traced back to their originators and then destroyed by destroying the originators. It is a very clever way to explain and destroy political ideas.

It is crucial that gossip be seen as a political and counterrevolutionary act. It is a means by which women can form hierarchies without interfering in men's hierarchies. It takes energy away from our real struggle, which is not just personal (in that it is not against individual people) but ideological and political. Gossiping about Richard Nixon will not bring him down, any more than gossping about a woman will build a movement which can destroy sexism. Furthermore, if the gossip were really concerned with the behavior of the victim, we would confront her instead of stabbing her in the back.

But the crucial point about gossips is that they attack political women without attacking their politics, when it is clearly their politics that are threatening. Straight women gossip about Lesbians in order to excuse themselves from dealing with Lesbianism. Reformists support gossips because they don't want to face either their own oppression or responsibility for their own actions. They don't want to face the fact that they do not fight their oppression. If you understand your oppression then you are faced with the moral decision of complying with it or fighting to end it. Apolitical women want to hide from that decision; gossips help them do it by smearing the women who would force that decision upon them. Men adore gossips because it weakens the entire movement and keeps them in the power seat longer.

We should be clear about the difference between gossip and political fights. Gossip is not ideological struggle. Gossip is under-the-table verbal assassination. Gossip serves our enemies by weakening us and making us look like backstabbing fools. Political differences exist and one way to educate ourselves is to air them. We owe it to ourselves to freely express those political differences. Reformism is different from revolution and any attempt to smooth over the sharp lines of divergence only water down the politics of both beliefs and make them sweetly liberal.

It is a mistake to assume that gossip is just talk, that women who gossip are merely prattling and that gossip does not have specific targets for specific reasons. A woman in the movement who gossips cannot be said to lack politics. She gossips about those whose politics are different from her own. Gossip therefore serves her political interests as well as her more petty concerns. She is able to rip to shreds a political person and avoid a confrontation with that person's political ideas. She insures that other women will not consider the analysis of the women she is damning. The sad fact is that people not only remain ignorant of the purpose of this behavior, they are influenced by it.

The values that operate in gossip are those that operate in any power struggle. The gossip is seeking a measure of power for herself with the least amount of risk possible. She tries to enlarge and defend her personal or semi-political power over those that threaten it. The more powerful a person's political analysis, the more viciously must this kind of woman attack her. Gossip gives you control over others and when facing gossip we often forget this basic fact--control.

The question now is what to do about gossip. If you are the object of political attacks, covered as gossip, you can try to short circuit the gossip by speaking straight out. She will probably evade you, cry, or try to lie her way out. You can confront her in front of other people so that they can judge what is going down. One amazing upshoot of this procedure may be that after this exchange is over, the gossip will gather her followers and twist the entire exchange to her own advantage. A ripe lie is that she was too overcome with emotion (that old trick again) to respond. Horseshit.

If you cannot stop the chief initiator, you can at least stop the cycle from spreading by calling your group together (be it consciousness raising, a project group, or a tightly organized cell) and making everyone aware of the problem. Everyone should understand that not only is someone's character being assassinated, but that the political ideas of that person, and by extension, the group with which she works, are being destroyed.

The most effective way to deal with gossips is to cut out their tongues. However, at this time, that is not feasible. Gossips can bad rap you from coast to coast and they can succeed in slowing down your work because other people who don't yet know you will be leery of you. But if you are seriously trying to change the conditions we all live in, no amount of gossip can cover that seriousness over. *Keep Working.* In time, even some of the former supporters of a gossip will clearly see who gets the work done and who doesn't--and no amount of psychological hogwash can obscure why the gossip can't get anything together, including herself.

Keep your head up and don't stoop to answer her ridiculous accusations and outright lies. The future is yours. Her future is to fall in the trashcan of the struggle against sexism.

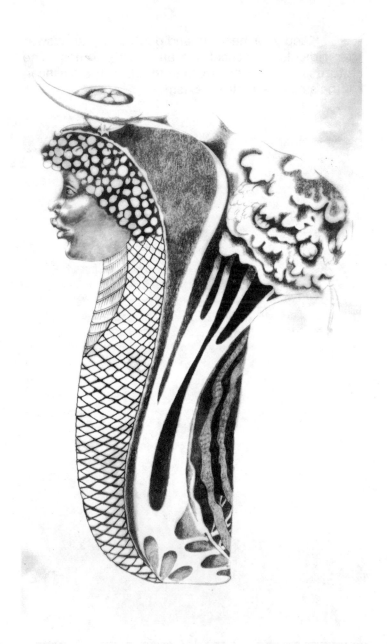

Leadership vs. Stardom

The Lesbian Movement and the Women's Liberation Movement have confused leaders with stars. From this confusion, as well as others, an anti-leadership attitude has half paralyzed these two movements.

First, the difference between a star and a leader should be made clear. A star is a woman acclaimed a "leader" by the white, rich, male media establishments. In this category fall such individuals as Kate Millet, Betty Friedan, Gloria Steinem, Germaine Greer and others. A star has little or no political following. She has done something that the media finds noteworthy--written a book, founded a reformist organization, made a public fool of herself, etc. She serves male supremacy by being a token. For this service she is often rewarded financially, socially and in terms of ego as it has developed in male society. She justifies her scabbing by declaring she reaches millions of women through the existing media institutions. In fact, she does, but her message is no real threat to white, rich, male political power. She may upset Norman Mailer and individual men but she does not upset, even momentarily, the balance of power.

The star is not allowed by men to use their

More and more working class women of all races are tasting a forbidden fruit: individualism.

media for the purpose of creating a revolution (do you think Chiang K'ai Chek would have let Mao use his newspapers?)--so the star fills apolitical women with bogus politics that suit male purposes. After viewing a star on t.v. a woman (according to the star's side of the story) has had her consciousness raised. She, the viewer, can then struggle with her individual man for concessions or even join a reformist Women's Liberation group. The star misdirects women into activities that keep men in power by, at best, challenging them piecemeal, i.e., the abortion movement, child care--those movements are simply feminist trade unionism. The male power base is never challenged except perhaps in rhetoric. Not only does the star keep men in power, she keeps women from a revolutionary understanding of woman oppression as well as other forms of oppression in this country. How can the star do otherwise--she would lose her token status and the rewards she has become accustomed to. She is handpicked by men to represent women the way they want women represented. Her future is tied into their future.

Beguiled by the star, women pin their hopes on the flickering t.v. image rather than looking for the answer among themselves or in looking toward a leader for the direction that will help themselves. Stars maintain traditional passivity in women. Worse, the star has the seal of male approval, she is "legitimate" so women listen to her before they listen to a true leader in their own hometown who gets no approval from the male power structure. Stars give women the illusion of involvement; true leaders demand commitment. A woman doesn't have to deal with the star, politically or personally, but with the grass roots leader she has the possibility of a flesh and blood relationship. Stars, then, keep women from each other.

A simple rule of thumb for stars is this: she gets money, approval and status from the white, rich, male world. Do you think she is going to destroy male supremacy? How can she--she's on their payroll. The star must denounce Lesbian-feminist politics, sweep them under the rug in a gesture of bisexual liberalism or ridicule those politics in order to make them more unacceptable to women. If the star doesn't do these things, men will get someone who does. The star performs these acts now and she will do them much more in the future. The stronger we get, the more attacks or snide dismissals we can expect--before millions of women. In plain words: Men are using stars to destroy a women's revolution and the leaders of that revolution.

Who is the star? To date, she has been white, middle class, well-educated and based in New York City, media captial of the United States. In the future we can expect her to assume other geographies and identities. Also in the future, we can expect some of these women, i.e., Betty Friedan, to share in white, capitalist power but these tokens will in no way change the structure of government nor of the economy. All they will change is the sexual balance, a surface change which has the potential of fooling apolitical women into thinking that real changes are possible.

Most women inside the Lesbian Movement and the Women's Liberation Movement have recognized the sellout of stars. Knowing the danger of star behavior, women have attacked the stars. Their attacks play into the hands of the male supremacists who then use the "fact" that "women hate each other and can't work together." It's a set up from start to finish. The stars exploit other women and slow down real political development. Political women realize this, rightfully attack the stars and then are exploited by men who use this against the movement, against all women--and in the face of the entire nation since they control the t.v., newspapers and radios.

If this is the behavior of the stars, what is the behavior of the leaders? How do we define a leader, especially since that work calls up visons of loudmouthed, pushy ego-centered men? A leader, for us, is a woman who comes from the ranks of the movement. She works hard, has probably been responsible for political analysis and/or program. She is not receiving rewards from male supremacists to divert our movement. Hopefully, she will feel good about her work but she shouldn't get egotistical about it. She doesn't emotionally manipulate women to get them on her "side." She moves forward with ideas and programs that develop from those ideas. She knows that without a thorough analysis of the forces of oppression we cannot find the way to end that oppression. The leader knows that each woman must come to understand that analysis, advance it and become a leader herself. So the true leader is intensely concerned with helping other women become leaders. Leaders as individual women will not be carbon copies of the traits mentioned above but each leader should contain some of those traits and most importantly, determination. She has made the decision to use her life to fight her oppression. Unless millions of us make that same decision, leaders will be cut down by stars and physically cut down by men. It is a decision that each one of us must face or fall back from at some point in our lives.

Aside from being confused with stars, there are deeper and more disturbing reasons for the attack on leaders. These reasons are rooted in the white, middle class nature of part of the Lesbian Movement and most of the Women's Liberation Movement. Many women in those two movements are white and middle class and correctly aware of how individualism (every man for himself) and opportunism are the cornerstones of middle class training. They equate stardom with opportunism and they are right. However, when they apply this same equation to leadership it produces disastrous results; it destroys the future of those two movements.

These young women have attempted to institute a reign of equality within the movement which has, in practice, become a tyranny of personal conformity. Imagination, inspiration and efficient political organization are suspect and throttled.

This mistake is based in the middle class emphasis on psychology. Middle class women focus on a psychological interpretation of women oppression and male supremacy. This analysis forces them to concentrate on personal behavior rather than political analysis and action. In fact, one of the sacrosanct lines coming from this psychological emphasis is, "Your personal life is political." I am not arguing with that concept as I happen to believe it. What I am arguing against is how that concept has been misused. A woman's personal life is all that men have left to her since she has no political life within their structures. (Some women have successful careers but they are an exception, you can't base your analysis on exceptions.) Women can become emotional virtuosos as they have few other outlets except bullshit jobs if they are middle class and shit jobs if they are working class. The first step for many women in recognizing their oppression is to examine their personal lives. The fault occurs when they remain there after a number of months, even years. This concern with the personal life keeps women in their circumscribed territory. Women become obsessed with the issues of monogamy, collective living, one to one relationships with other women, etc. and they do not link these concerns to political organization and action. In keeping with this lack of connection is the truism, coming again out of a psychological analysis, which is that if you love women you will mysteriously destroy male supremacy and end your oppression. Oppression is not analyzed in terms of economic and political power hence it is not fought on those levels. And so the two movements remain right where men want them--circling around women's personal lives, safely away from the seat of male power. A woman who begins to understand power and what must be done about it becomes suspect by other women. She becomes a leader, takes the initiative, pushes other women to understand oppression in power terms as well as psychological terms. The other women fear that the leader is operating on a vertical scale (the way men do) so they feel beneath her. The tremendous self-hatred that smoulders within every oppressed breast then gets focused on the leader. She is feared for her development, envied for her togetherness and hated for her guts. Also, she is much easier to attack than the oppressor so she provides some relief from the frustrations that accompany oppression.

Women make the mistake of comparing themselves to the leader instead of learning from her and becoming leaders themselves. Isn't it natural enough for women to compare themselves to other women? Men encourage this as a way to keep women worried as to whether they make the grade when competing for men. It's a mistake to carry over this behavior. It is oppressed behavior rather than behavior designed to end oppression.

The irony of this anti-leadership, anti-individualism mood that has swept the two movements is that it has spawned a distorted form of the very individualism it set out to combat: countless isolated groups composed of individuals intent on their own personal lives and the lives of others in their group. When each woman's personal life or the interaction of her group becomes more important than a national political program to free all women it is a guarantee that a cohesive political movement cannot emerge. Small groups are dedicated to going in their own direction, the only thing uniting them is their individualism. When small groups go their own way regardless of how it affects other groups or the movement as a whole you have nothing but destructive chaos. It isn't that individual women and small groups are deliberately sabotaging a national movement. It is that they have not seriously analyzed political power so they can't think in terms beyond their own lives and the lives of women around them. Innocent in their ignorance, these women maintain male supremacy as well as class and race oppression.

The anti-leadership propaganda also maintains women who control groups by emotional manipulation. Face it, women are suckers for this trick. A torrent of tears at the critical moment and an entire group of women can be subverted from their political work. One of the horrors of woman oppression is that women personalize ideas and fight out ideas through personalities. What better way to stay oppressed than to continue to confine women to emotionalism? What better way to control women than to appeal to their emotions? As it is, the leaders who advance political thought and action are the people singled out for personalization. They are gossiped about and destroyed by the emotional manipulators. Their ideas are submerged by attacks on their personalities. Since the emotional manipulator is so hard for women to track down, especially since middle class women are practically blind to this kind of behavior since they are reared in it--it takes months, even years, for women to realize they've been duped by a manipulator and in that time they may have contributed to the destruction of a grass roots leader.

The emotional manipulators serve male supremacy by keeping women from doing any real work, keeping their attention fixed on personalities and psychological problems, by passing that off as political analysis and by keeping women from true leaders, fostering confusion and hatreds that waste our energies and weaken us.

I'm not declaring that emotions are to be suppressed. We are women, not insensitive clods. But emotion has been our woman's place and it has been used against us. We must become more concerned with political analysis and actions which channel our emotions and strengthen us personally rather than concentrating on our individual feelings and wallowing in them. We must painstakingly, logically develop a political program growing from our ideology and our lives. Emotionalism has yet to produce a just government--historically it has given us The Terror, Hitler's concentration camps and Stalin's Great Purge.

A few leaders have recognized the dangers of emotionalism, recognized the need for political ideology and program, and from that, a party.

These women have been effectively bottled up and kept from developing that party by the anti-leadership elements in the movements and the paid pigs, who are squeezing anti-leadership for all they can get. The anti-leadership women have both contempt and fear for the idea of an organized party, cooperative action. This fear is a contradiction of the process of revolution. The great revolutions of this century have been built by political parties not by stars and anarchists. The failure of those revolutions for all their innovations lies in their sexist basis, male supremacy was never questioned, half the population still enslaved the other half when the revolution was over. But the *process* of revolution remains a realistic way to change power. I'm not advocating a rerun of any prior revolution but there are lessons for us in history, especially if we can speed up our own development by picking up on the good things they did.

We'll never have the chance to smash sexism if we don't form a party. We can't survive politically without a party and for women to assume that our party will be an imitation of male parties is another betrayal of womankind—they don't believe in women, they don't believe we can build new structures. They add to that betrayal, cowardice: they aren't going to take any risks, they aren't going to commit themselves to finding a real way to end our oppression. They will sit back and cut us to ribbons, secure in their moral vanity.

The irony of this fear and contempt is that it is, again, rooted in individualism of the destructive variety. These women proclaim rosy anarchy, spontaneity, feeling high. All women will be leaders according to them yet they block the emergence of leaders at every turn. According to the theorists of instant revolution, all you have to add is feeling and there will be a change in political power because of an "organic" process. This is never defined but feeling good is part of it and talking about yourself incessantly seems to strengthen that original assumption. This trumpeted ignorance of the political structure we are up against is astonishing. It can only come from class privilege which shields people from the ugly realities of power in America. To the hawkers of instant revolution, organized long term struggle is repugnant and discipline is unthinkable. They fear that organization and discipline (which means that you sometimes think of others before you think of yourself) will lose them the autonomy that a middle class, psychological analysis has set them up to expect. What autonomy is available under the political structures of white, rich, heterosexual male supremacists unless it be at the expense of your sisters--sisters who are not middle class, not heterosexual and not white.

Perhaps some of this anti-leader, anti-party sentiment comes from the fact that middle class people are traditionally concerned with playing it safe. If you are going to combat your oppression you are no longer safe. Part of it also comes from middle class life where people usually didn't need to band together to survive, they fought each other constantly for more material rewards. A party demands that you band together on a political level.

Since World War I, family structures have weakened in all the classes, more jobs have opened up to women, even working class women, and this has given working class women some of the personal freedom that her more privileged sisters enjoyed, at the price of destroying much of the old working class sense of togetherness. In some cases, it is beginning to destroy class identity among younger women. More and more working class women of all races are tasting a forbidden fruit: individualism.

Many working class, young women have entered the movement with a fierce sense of personal freedom and a heightened awareness of class oppression for those who did not forget class identity. Others have bought middle class values and greatly add to the confusion over class in the movements. Those women who resisted the middle class values which are destructive are determined to fight those values. This determination doubles when they are faced with the blind oppression of the white, middle class woman. Many of these working class women reject leadership because it has meant to them getting fucked over by middle class women. Those whose class identity has been blurred follow the line of least resistance which is to go along with the middle class women who attack leaders for all the reasons stated in this article. These blurred women, imitators of the middle class, are then used as tokens by the real middle class women the same way men use women as tokens to keep themselves in power. Whenever a middle class woman wants to destroy a leader, especially a working class leader, she uses another working class woman to attack her.

No matter where the anti-leadership comes from, it must be stopped, just as star rip offs must be stopped. Both forces destroy our movement and aid male supremacy.

We stop stars not by attacking them but by concentrating on reaching other women. This is why the development of a strong women's media is essential. At times you will explain to a new woman what stardom means politically but that's all the time we need spend on stars. Our time must be spent in action with women, not in reaction to women controlled by men.

As for anti-leadership, we stop it by becoming politically realistic and also by calling it loud and clear when we see a leader getting lynched. We are not all alike, nor should we be, that's what men have tried to do to us, make us all alike--it's a repeat of that horror story to do it to each other. Some of us will be leaders in developing political theory, others in action, and other women will lead in medicine, acting, music and hundreds of other areas. Each woman will discover what she can do for herself and for the movement through her talents. The point is not that we *be* alike but that we *share* a common political ideology and program and we use our individual talents in those programs to free us all. If we cannot do this then we will stay oppressed and death will remain the theme song of this world sung in a chorus of bass voices.

The Last Picture Show

If *The Last Picture Show* were the last picture show to have as its theme the life and times of a young man on the "verge of maturity," I would view it with less jaundice. However, the coming-of-age movie seems entrenched; men are apparently fascinated with their first fuck and with the fading of boyhood into what is euphemistically termed "manhood." This particular movie, saturated with packaged cinematic sensitivity, is more dishonest than most in its handling of a hackneyed theme.

First: the technical dishonesty: movies shot in black and white in the 1970's are artsy fartsy. Human beings see in color; we don't need to be insulted by enduring a black and white movie which is to clue us in on the fact that it is "serious." There's a class aspect to black and white movies in our times. Supposedly, the bleak screen will serve to heighten the viewer's sense of the drab, the working class, the Impoverished.

Those of us growing up impoverished were oppressed in living color and any deviation from that is a perversion of our lives justified in terms of "style." When our ceilings peeled they peeled from pea green to red to black to grey and all together it was more hideous than anything shot in black and

Is there a way out of this rot, this media sabotage of our lives?

white. The only possible excuse any filmmaker can offer for shooting in black and white is money. Anything else is elevated crap.

If the color insult were not enough, we had to endure bad lighting, zilch camera work and shots of the Texas plain held overlong.

The shabby technical work is collaborated with the shabby story line which is the archetypical relationship: two male friends. This time it's Sonny and Duane. Let's follow Sonny and Duane in their adventures. So we do. They get drunk. They hurt a deaf-dumb friend. They screw girls. They fight each other. From these activities Sonny's "manhood" emerges, an understanding of life. No, I'm not making this up--if you've seen the movie, you know it's true. Why do people sit through this shit? It's very simple and it's all connected with male supremacy, white supremacy, and class supremacy.

The people who make movies are male, white, usually middle class and usually heterosexual. The people who review the movies for the most part bear those same distinctive scars. So the rest of us who don't fit into those categories have to watch movies that have nothing to do with our lives. Worse, we have no access to media to communicate the reality of our own life experiences. Therefore all of America since the beginning of film has had to watch the white, middle class, heterosexual male version of life. I don't know about you, but I'm sick of it.

If white men had concentrated only on themselves it wouldn't be so disastrous, but they didn't. They gave us their version of what women are, what Blacks are, what people are who are not like themselves. It's grim. Women, sex objects, live through men. Blacks in the 30's and 40's were happy, dancing, simple people. Today, Blacks are superstud detectives treating women the way white men treat women. Those distortions, past and present, have influenced oppressed people, influenced us to a harmful degree. All too often, oppressed people identified with the oppressor's definition of themselves, an activity which creates intense self-hatred, hatred of your own kind and a desire to "make it" in the rich, white man's world. People denied their own *life experience* and adopted the media image of life as fact.

The Last Picture Show successfully meets most of our oppression ratings. It ignores Texas' racial question completely; the movie is 100% white; non-white existence isn't even verbally recognized; it presents an arty version of working class whites as well as the typical male supremacist view of women. And this film gets rave reviews from most critics plus "right on" from the radical community.

To draw a sharper focus on the distortion, the women characters in the movie are worth a look. All the women in the movie are vacant and what little there is of life for them revolves around the men. Not one of these women has work of her own or even a hobby. Now many Texan women in the 1950's may have been that vacuous, but they did have some brains in their heads even if they didn't have careers or hobbies. In *The Last Picture Show* they do not have brains in their heads, just dim ghosts of intelligence.

Jacy, the beautiful young girl, is a spiteful bitch who pits the boys against each other. No insights as to why she does that, of course. We only see poor Duane and Sonny suffering. Most women reading this article know why Jacy does what she does. Men, however, are disturbed and mystified by this "bitch behavior." That's all we know of

Jacy, bitchiness; her character is not developed, we see only surface action. I didn't take this lack of character development as sexist because the characters of the men didn't get off the ground either. Cybill Shepard deserves a great deal of credit for taking a tedious teenager and holding our attention with her.

Jacy's mother, played by Ellen Burstyn, is more interesting. She is good-looking, late thirties-early forties, bored as hell with Texas, her husband, her tacky lover. She knows sex doesn't mean much when you do it with men and she makes this clear although I doubt that was the intention of the author or the director. Lois is the only person in the film who sees through the heterosexual sham, but unfortunately, she doesn't see far enough, the usual film lobotomy on female minds. So Lois wanders through the movie trying to convey her experiences to her daughter in order to save her from the same faded life. Too bad she didn't wander into her local, neighborhood Lesbian, it might have made a better movie and Lois would have been a much happier woman.

Bogdanovich's (McMurty's) portrayal of the women isn't even outrageous, it's dreary and familiar. What is outrageous is that people are still receptive to that conception of women.

Sexism explains why men view women in the same old way, but what explains how they view themselves? Do they actually think that Sonny and Ben the Lion are sensitive men? Why hasn't this sentimental slop about white, male, small town youth been rejected by critical male reviewers? Worse, if it is a fairly honest portrayal of those youths, then men are much worse off than I thought. The men in this movie are not sensitive to anything except what is connected to their concept of self. They have zero ability to empathize with a woman's life and only the tiniest ability to empathize with each other.

Even the two men closest to each other, Sonny and Duane, do not understand and love each other. Each man is locked into his sense of himself which, according to *The Last Picture Show,* is tied into screwing girls/women. If that's what men's lives are like we can look forward to World War III unless there is a women's revolution. Unfeeling, unthinking, uncaring about anything except their concept of self, "masculinity," these men are set-ups for any politician or military leader who can give them that "butch" self they crave. If anyone doubts the severity of this collective male identity crisis and its potential for political manipulation remember that Hitler built a party out of the same psychological dynamic.

The only time in the movie when a male character is not centered on himself, when he is drawn into another human life, is at death. When Billy is killed, Sonny recognizes a love for the deaf-dumb boy. Is death what it takes to get men to realize they love somebody? And running true to form, Billy's death was too much for Sonny to handle so he ran to a woman to help him get through it. And she ran true to form according to white, heterosexual moviemakers--she was glad to help him, even though he had fucked her over. She threw a five-minute fit, cried and took him back. What incredible male propaganda. With this kind of propaganda on the screen, do you ever wonder if the moviemakers are part of the ruling elite's plot to keep us all down?

The Last Picture Show, like all pictures made in this country, feeds us a distortion of life, feeds us an apolitical, hopeless view of the world. And that apolitical view is the only view available to the public in mass form. Movies may be critical of American life, *The Last Picture Show* is certainly that, but the subject matter has been flogged to death. It's a catechism and audience reaction is automatic. There is nothing new, challenging or useful. It provides mechanized outlet for frustration with no solution. There seems to be a shred of reality on the screen, after all, most white, middle class viewers came out of spiritual, emotional emptiness if we are to believe their testimonies in the arts and politics, so they are safe in the familiar, dressed-up to look different, i.e. working class Texans--but they haven't been pushed, questioned, taught.

These movies are more than apolitical or neutral, they are blocks to real political understanding. *The Last Picture Show* offers no analysis of why people's lives are empty. The screen in America is kept free from disquieting political thought, although it is kept entertaining. This absence of thought, analysis, solution gives us barrenness frequently disguised in technical riches.

More, movies serve the oppressors in ways other than diverting us from thought, movies offer mild protest without resolution, catharsis without cure. Movies keep images of oppressed people intact and relative to the image of the white, middle class male. The oppressed image only changes (if at all) if the white, male image changes--i.e., Dustin Hoffman in *The Graduate* and *Midnight Cowboy.*

These changes are so minute that we can safely say racism, classism and sexism reign supreme in the movies. *The Last Picture Show* is not *Green Beret,* which is blatant enemy propaganda. *The Last Picture Show* is more destructive because it is so seductive to the minds of white, middle class males and the heterosexual women still tied to that system of thinking/acting/being--and that's millions of men.

The seduction is based on the ignorance mentioned earlier in the article. Without an understanding of other people's lives, the white, middle class heterosexual viewer finds her/his experience reinforced by the media and is never confronted by those of us coming from very different places. The movies may seem honest because the viewer can pick out parts of her/his experience which corresponds to it. But to millions of us who are the "Other," those movies are white men's lies, lies we have to fight every day in our existence. Even the parts of a movie, this movie, which are honest cannot soften the overall effect of the movie: it keeps us in our place, our place in the movie, in the media, which is no place.

Is there a way out of this art rot, this media sabotage of our lives? Yes, but it's a long haul and the critical element is not drive, talent, or skills, but money. We have to make our own films. We have to convey the truth of our own life experiences to the mass public.

I would like to think we could all get it together and do it. But who is going to give us the money to make high quality, well distributed movies? Our vision of the world, our thoughts are threatening to the people who control the money, the government and obliquely, the film industry. We have a vibrant. newborn art. How can we get it to the public?

However we do it, we must do it. Film is a powerful form of communication and we need it. We have to build a fighting media or we will find our ideas in twisted form selling vaginal deodorant before 1980 as well as selling us down the river. We have to build a media to get across a few scraps of the truth, of our lives, our art and of a hope beyond violent despair.

The Last Picture Show will not be the last oppressor's movie we will watch. But it can be the last picture show we watch passively. Get yourself together and help build our own media. Write, paint, dance, speak, sing, act--it doesn't matter what you do as long as you do something. I know that's not the whole answer but in my simple way, I can't but think that if each of us does something it will be a beginning.

A Manifesto for the Feminist Artist

Art in the past has been the pursuit of the privileged with few exceptions. It has been white, male, usually middle to upper class, and overwhelmingly heterosexual. All forms of the arts--music, dance, literature, painting, film, etc.--reflect the concerns of this dominant group with a few male homosexuals thrown in for good measure. Only recently have the concerns of other people and their art begun to emerge, especially within the Black community, and, in its beginning stages, among women.

Today 90% of what is available to the public remains the art of the oppressor. Since they control the business end of the arts they control what is presented to people. Therefore precious little of our work leaks out to the mass public. But their art for all its dominance is in such decline it has reached the final stages of disease and decadence. That art offers us two poles: nostalgia and porno-violence. Both come from emptiness, starvation of creativity and hope, and incredible self-indulgence.

Their concept of self has become so perverted that older members of the oppressor generation seek the coordinates of their fragmented selves on a graph of the past, nostalgia. Meanwhile the

The male ego is so eroded that. . .younger men. . .the inheritors of the political

younger generation gluts itself in an orgy of porno-violence. The male ego is so eroded that these younger men--the inheritors of the political-economic reins of the death culture--seek an affirmation of self in violent, destructive sex. Porno-violence is their symbol of protest that in its essence denies not only dignity and equality to women but even *life* to women. Rape is the cliche of male art, be it individual rape or the systematic brutalization of an entire sex and entire races.

As women artists we are in deep revolt against this rotting art just as we are in revolt against the syphilitic political structures that damage us and endanger world peace.

Our experiences have been locked away from the eyes and ears of the people. We must fight to transmit those experiences forcing people to face the reality of our lives, of all oppressed people's lives. But our art must be more than personal narrative; it must contain a vision for the future where no group rapes another, where force is not the heart of politics and egotism not the mind of art.

Our task is to achieve a synthesis of poetry and politics, theater and experience, love and society. We have to pull together a world compartmentalized by the resident schizophrenics in the White House, the Pentagon and General Motors. We have to build our own media, a new art to help us create a new government in which all

economic reins of the death culture. . .seek an affirmation of self in violent, destructive sex.

people are free. Let our work be the bridge to that
new world.

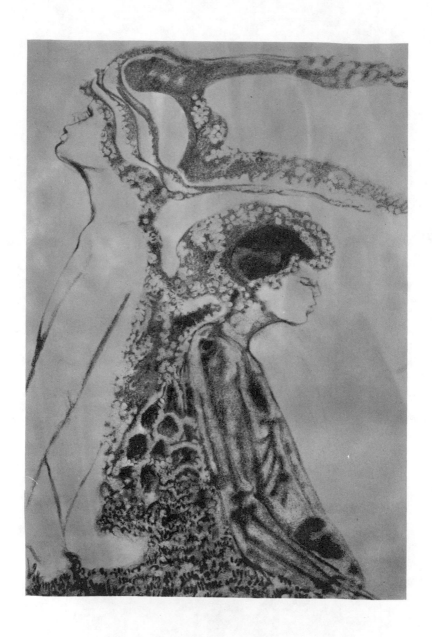

Love Song for Feminists from Flamingo Park

The Miami Women's Coalition invited me to the Republican counter-convention to be part of Women in Revolt, billed as the day when "We will come to demand the freedom to determine our own lives." This was to culminate in a rally where we could celebrate women's culture. What I found was anything but women in revolt and zero women's culture. To be blunt, the entire day was co-opted by male-defined issues.

The women sabotaged themselves by not allowing any leadership to emerge within the women's caucus. Another victory for false egalitarianism which left them particularly vulnerable to disruption. And disrupted they were. First, by the Zipples who managed to offend everyone. Secondly, by random men who sniffed at the women's tent like dogs around bitches in heat. The Romeos at the tent were better than the deliberately vulgar men on the campgrounds who went out of their way to verbally and in some instances, physically, harrass women. Thirdly, the women were disrupted by the overall leadership (mostly white, middle class males) of the counter-convention. These gentlemen have so little understanding of sexism that they allowed the anti-rape squads to be treated as a joke by the entire

The left is dying by its own hand.

campsite.

Most women at the women's tent were "new" women. They drifted to the counter-convention to search for an answer but which answer? To a woman they were dedicated to ending the war, and so am I. The war may end and if it does it will be greatly due to the work of the left. But the behavior that causes wars will still exist and this behavior is found among men on the left as much as it is found among Nixon and his cronies.

How this behavior can affect people was apparent at the women's rally. The march to the rally site was all women. It was spirited, even joyful. Once gathered at the site a fantastic women's rock band, the Grapevine, played and it was wonderful to listen to good music by women. The rally was open to men and they filtered into the crowd. When the speaking began the 1000 (rough estimate) people were pretty evenly divided between men and women. The women sat on the ground while most of the men stood on the perimeter of this circle, arms folded, not sullen but not joyful. The mood of the rally shifted. What was to be a celebration of women's culture was just another male left front with women as principal speakers. All it really meant was that women got up and spoke out against the war, the government, instead of male heavies doing all the talking.

Unfortunately, I was to be one of those speakers. I wanted to celebrate women's culture and had prepared myself to read poetry and fire away at sexism. I had no idea in hell that men were going to attend that rally. Aside from that shock I was the lone feminist and the only overt lesbian. When I got up and looked out over those beautiful women's faces, I felt sick. The rally was all safely on the anti-war, talk-about-what-men-think-is-important groove. Behind the women as if containing them by their bodies was a wall of beards. The first rows of those seated were taken over by the VietNam Veterans Against the War for security reasons. The Nazis and right-wing Cubans were going to march by the site during Jane Fonda's and Erica Huggins' speeches. Another slap in the face, we can't take care of ourselves. This move was certainly not done by the veterans to irritate women. The leadership of the convention may have agreed to it or the veterans fearing trouble, may have just moved in.

If I gave a feminist speech I would have incriminated the men at the counter-convention as well as the administration even if I didn't say it directly. Was I going to do this in front of the establishment media which will use any opportunity to smear any of the movements? The Zippies were giving them enough rotten coverage. Angry as I am at the male left I am not going to vent my anger in front of a slicker brand of pig. Although the left treats us despicably, we still should have a measure of loyalty in face of a larger enemy. There was also the very real consideration that if I hit hard on sexism and the subversion of the women's rally, I would have added to the tensions already existing within the camp, exposing other women to increased hostility or putting them in the position of having to explain themselves in relation to my attack. To complete the scenario I was introduced as a lesbian poet. The women cheered. Most of the men did not. I tried with no success to skirt the conflict and obligatory rhetoric, to inject some political humor into the rally. Had the rally been for women only it might have worked even given the preceding speakers--articulate women speaking on ''accepted'' issues. But I was out of luck. I gutted my whole speech, ran through the essentials in four minutes and got two laughs out of it.

Jane Fonda spoke next. A spectacularly gifted woman she did speak about women, the Vietnamese women. The feminist connections were missing. Since I had an opportunity to discover that this woman is truly fine and warm and, for a lack of a better word, good, I feel even more unhappy about her. One more beautiful sister we are kept from by men and their politics which deny our own.

The rally also confirmed my suspicions about the crowd format as a method for communication. The "mass rally" is a form ripe for manipulation, a set-up for cheap emotionalism. I am not trying to give sly hints that the other speakers were cheap emotionalists. They displayed integrity but even the most self-contained speaker cannot help but be shaped by the silent demands of the crowd. When those crowds are full of left men the expectation is for overstatement and revolutionary jargon. The crowd wants its guilt washed away in sanguine rhetoric that makes its struggle look as heroic as the Vietnamese. It wants heroism so it can hide its pathetic helplessness in the mirror of grandeur. It wants Nixon so it can bypass the difficult process of pulling apart policies and coming up with workable, more compassionate forms of government. It wants paper challenges for international peace while it ignores the poor in our own backyard. It wants illusions of solidarity without the sweat of compromise, change and consciousness raising that are the heart of coalition politics. And it is that illusion of solidarity which the women's rally gave the crowd at the expense of women.

Yes, the Vietnamese are dying. I know that. Women are dying here every day because they were born women but the left doesn't know or doesn't want to know. The Vietnamese have been fighting the rape of their land for centuries. We have been fighting rape for over 10,000 years. Our deaths are in the multi-millions. Our deaths are "unglamorous," "individual" and shorn of the cloak of heroism. We are not attacked by a uniformed army. We are stalked by seemingly ordinary men. Our enemy is an army of neighbors.

One more example of the left's shabby disregard for sexism as a political issue was the Senior Citizens Investigation. They conducted a two-day investigation into the policies of Nixon's administration. They did not want me to appear but combined pressure from the women's and gay caucuses won out but only if I appeared for women. I didn't. As best I could, I took on the entire issue of sexism, its effect on women, lesbians, gay and straight men and how sexist policy serves any administration. All in one hour. It was an outrage that there weren't speakers to cover all these aspects of sexism, that the only speaker who dealt with the issues was shuttled to the last place on the program so she could be conveniently missed. It was also an underhanded way to ignore the gay men who had been subject to ridicule all during the counter-convention.

This inability of the male left to deal with sexism (along with racism and class) has trapped them into a narrow politics that is becoming increasingly ineffectual. The counter convention was a shadow of earlier times. You'd think by now the left would realize it's disintegrating and one reason is that you don't organize people by being hostile to their needs.

Despite the "official" troubles at Flamingo Park there were moments of happiness on that scrap of sand. Those moments renewed my commitment to the potential of women. I want to especially thank a sister with blue eyes who corrected me after the investigation when I took a potshot at straight women. She did this out of concern, not as a put-down, and I learned from her. Thank you to Edda and Beth who took responsibility for me and other women because they love women. Thanks to Gerri and Mae who endured my complaint and who decided to stick it out even though the women had been sold out. Thank you to Jane Fonda who could have pulled a classic straight lady number and steered clear of the lesbian lest she be guilty by association--but she didn't. And thank you to a slender, blond man who cheered me in Wolfie's restaurant and who went out of his way to greet me at the campsite. Those were the times we came through for each other as human beings...the moments when we are closest to discovering that we need to build a powerful force to fight this inhuman government. And those are the moments buried by left politics.

The issues dwarf the people. In that respect the left is no different than the establishment. It is that difference which convinces me that we "outcasts" from the left, for all our stumbling, are on the right track. We know that once you deny a person a self it is a step away from denying life. We have been denied selves in the system only to be denied selves in the male left. For us--the women, lesbians, gay men--the individual comes first.

Years ago when Women's Liberation said the personal is political I nodded "yes" and dimly understood it. The counter-convention drove that concept into my gut. If we lose the individual in the face of a "larger" issue, if we ignore someone who is perhaps not "charismatic" or articulate, we play out the deadly behavioral patterns that culminate internationally in imperialism and interpersonally in rape.

When are women going to withdraw their support from those patterns of behavior and stop funneling their phenomenal energies into the cesspool of male politics? When are women going to put themselves on the line for each other and build the culture we can build, a culture that resists the butchery of the self and the mutilation of the flesh?

Sisters, we have the answers. Each of us is a piece of the puzzle which when put together is the blueprint for a new society. What are we doing farting around and allowing ourselves the luxury of disillusionment?—Allowing the pig divisions of class, race and lesbianism to divide us? Are we going to dissipate ourselves in internal struggles or emerge as a powerful political force? The left is dying by its own hand. We are the only force that can stop the poisonous dance of power that erupts in Viet Nam or in Flamingo Park.

I Am A Woman

Any woman who tries to do something, be it political or artistic , deserves credit. Viveca Linfors as the sole actress in *I Am A Woman* currently at Arena Stage therefore deserves a certain amount of credit. The temptation of this reviewer is to give her more credit than she deserves, pretend it was a fine show and make everyone feel good with dishonest praise. Criticizing men is easy. Criticizing women is painful. Yet we do each other a disservice as artists if we pretend it's all quite marvelous and we weaken the intellectual growth of the entire Women's Movement which has too long fed itself the nectar of easy applause.

I Am A Woman is a safe therefore boring show. Each of the many short pieces are strung together like a child's cutout dolls connected by the theme of heterosexuality. This piecemeal approach to drama is difficult to sustain because each part does not build on the other. Bouncing from Emilia of Shakespeare's *Othello* to Judy Syfers "I Want A Wife" isn't dislocating, it's debilitating. What the audience is left with is a handful of dramatic clips. The law of averages dictates that you'll like at least some of them and hopefully ignore the rest. However "the rest" comprised the bulk of the

A single performer drawing on a stable of authors is in serious trouble...

show.

The major weakness was the content. The short scenes were drawn mainly from literature, journalism and some drama. The authorship was roughly divided between male and female. From a feminist viewpoint this is theatrical liberalism we don't need. Every time we walk into a theatre, turn on the tube, sit in a movie house, we are forced to see the male concept of the female. That's the standard. If *I Am A Woman* desired to be the tiniest bit daring it would have drawn its material from women authors. We don't need to pay to hear Brecht on women. But to hear women on women-- that's news.

Far more disturbing than tokenism concerning authorship is the content itself. The entire evening was devoted to examining women's relationships with men. At the very bravest, there were a few little snips about women thinking on their own situation and identity--this usually in relation to men. Heterosexuality happens to be part of millions of women's lives. It is certainly the structure of every childhood. But even the most blatantly heterosexual woman has a relationship with her mother, her sisters, her girlfriends, aunts, grandmothers, office workers. *I Am A Woman* has one faint attempt at looking at a woman to woman relationship, so faint that one strains for the connection. That is Colette's piece, ''My Mother's House,'' in which an aging mother speaks to her daughter. But what does she speak about--how age has affected her and how she is nervously preparing for her son to come through the gate. Although the piece is addressed to another woman, the core of it is her flirtation with her son. ''That's it folks,'' to quote Porky Pig. That is the one, the only examination of women's relationships with each other in the show. Unfortunately for Viveca Linfors, Coleen Dewhurst performed that same piece on television and it was one of the few times television justified its existence. Dewhurst was superb. Linfors was not. If she had just bombed that one number it wouldn't be so bad, but she bungled far too many. It's difficult to know how much of the bungling is due to her and how much should be credited to the director. For instance, Ms. Linfors' body carriage rarely changed from piece to piece. She constantly flipped her shoulders and hips in a coquettish fashion that didn't accentuate the material but detracted from it. When she did change her posture the transition was so obvious and stereotyped that it was embarrassing--i.e., a stoop for age. Vocally she came down heavy on the "key lines" and left no space for subtlety. There was a mechanical pause after any line that should have been funny. Miserable props didn't help any of this. A pile of rocks on the left of the stage and another pile on the right were bisected by a strange phallic looking tree or whatever that apparition was. It served as symbol to the content. *I Am A Woman* would have done better with a bare stage.

Content and acting aside, part of the problem with *I Am A Woman* is that one-woman shows don't work anymore. Film and TV have killed the form. A single performer drawing on a stable of authors is in serious trouble without electronic help or visual movement to keep an audience riveted. Whether you deplore the eye's need for toys or whether you are totally absorbed into visual culture, the fact remains that audiences today are different than audiences before film. The advent of film, and especially TV, nearly killed intellectual content in film, the theatre, and who knows where else. People can't listen to the sequential development of ideas any longer. This new deficiency has its own apologists to convince us of its charms--McLuhan et al. Today it's action, action, action, preferably porno-violence. (Our politicians have followed suit.) The theatre, instead of revitalizing and offering an oasis for systematic thought, went along with the new fragmentation and developed what is known as the "cinematic" technique. Shows such as *Follies* were a smash in New York because in a sense they were compressed, live movies. Scene after scene flashes before you, made coherent by the movement of characters in and out of the "cuts"--see *Godspell*, *Jesus Christ Superstar*, *Hair* for further illumination. All these shows are fascinating for visual effect and compelling acting but forget thought. *I Am A Woman* for its flawed and cowardly content makes a stab at forcing the audience to think. A man or woman with zero feminist consciousness might examine a few moth-eaten assumptions thanks to this show. But given the format of the show, only those halfway converted would turn up in the first place. The Kreeger Theatre holds 500. The performance I attended had only 171 bodies in the chairs. To bring in the heathen you need razzle dazzle. Clearly, razzle dazzle takes money. Those with the coins (and we know who they are) don't back even mild shows like *I Am A Woman*. Think where that puts those of us who are writing, acting, painting, living The Real Thing?

I Am A Woman's one ghost of a chance was in the acting. Viveca Linfors has been tremendous in the past, but she isn't tremendous in this show. Lacking that, the show falls apart in both conception and execution.

On leaving the theatre another writer depressed at the show's falling apart confessed to me, "God, it was hideous but a lot of people liked it, so I guess it's OK." That rationale has always justified impoverished art or politics. It's a dangerous rationale. Look at it politically. Opinion polls tell us a lot of people like Nixon. Is this a justification for accepting him? Switch to art. Millions of Americans flipped out over violently anti-woman *Clockwork Orange*. Does that mean we shrug our shoulders and say "OK"? The fact that many people tolerated, even liked, *I Am A Woman* is sad proof of how far we feminists have to go. If audiences were familiar with our work, *I Am A Woman* would be unacceptable and maybe even insulting to them.

Which brings me to my "Delenda est Cathago." *We Must Create Our Own Media!* Good feminist theatre, literature, good anything is going to come from us. The establishment is not going to produce it for us. And when we produce it ourselves the establishment media is not going to finance, produce, distribute it. Not only is the establishment media not going to let us tell our truth, establishment articles will attack us in much the same way that party hacks attack Solzhenltsyn. Make your decision now to work with women, build, create our new art. Don't wait for an establishment actress to legitimize you. Many of you are as good if not better than Viveca Linfors. Develop your talent. Be energized by your strength. Support your sisters. Organize a media network. If you do that, who knows, our women's theatre may even have the guts to put in a little piece about women actually loving other women. Can you dig that?

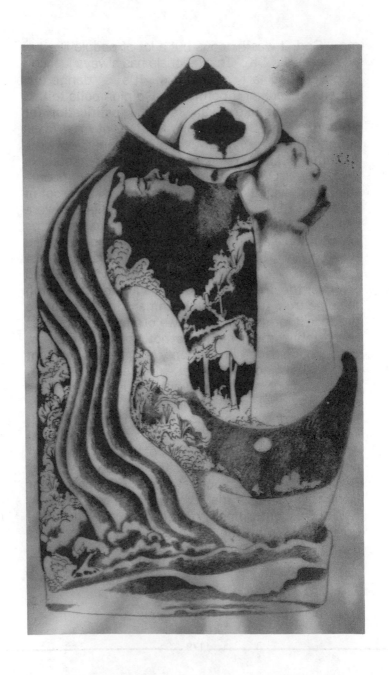

The Good Fairy

Remember the Good Fairy? She sprinkled dust on you and, poof, you changed into a beautiful princess or if you were bad, poof, you changed into a toad in need of weight watchers. Unfortunately, the Women's Liberation Movement can't locate the Good Fairy. If only we could find her, things would be so much easier. Rumor has it that she's shacked up with Santa Claus. My guess is she's off in Never-Never Land with Tinker Bell.

Both the Good Fairy and Santa Claus represent an attitude toward change which is dusturbing in its implications. Each rewards you for being "good" or "bad". Santa, the old capitalist (or is he a Bolshevik in all that red?), dumps material goodies on you. The Good Fairy, on the other hand, transforms your body or transports you to another land. Change is instantaneous. You can't really work for change as there is a strong element of luck attached to it. Process Is never mentioned, all we see is the end result--a princess, a fat toad or a Christmas tree surrounded by glittering packages.

The Good Fairy's not really to blame for the fact that we don't understand change. Over the centuries, women's lives have been peculiarly time-less, unchanged. We married, gave birth, raised

We desire and seek participation in the world and we do so without apology.

our children, bolstered our husbands. The few renegades from this unchanged and unchallenged condition usually were driven out of society, killed outright or lived double lives for fear of the above. Change as a personal and political reality is a dazzling new concept for women. We know we are changing. We don't always know how we are changing and we don't often know how to communicate that change and foster it in others. We face resistance not just from men, which we expect, but from other women, women frightened by us because we are so changed and because we can't tell them exactly how those changes came about. No wonder the Good Fairy would be such a help. A little dust and, poof, changed women and changed men: sisterhood and brotherhood.

Without such a magic wand, we need to come to grips with some tough problems. For one thing, history is not linear. Male supremacy does not stop and feminism begin. Feminism does not instantly change a woman into Sheena, Queen of the Jungle.

We can't blame ourselves too heavily for our surprise when the world didn't turn upside-down the day we became feminists. As Americans, we were taught peculiar ideas regarding change. The Good Fairy and Santa Claus, while being fun to consider, are serious symbols of those simplistic teachings. For instance, change is for better or for worse, it is emotional and moral, good or bad. We are not taught the concept of substitution, lateral motion, putting B in place of A with little substantive difference. For reasons worthy of an entire book on the subject, Americans have tremendous difficulty with gradations in quality, subtlety, complexity. An event, a person, a change is good or bad. Period.

We are largely unaware of process. While

most feminists, compared to other Americans, are sensitive to process, we too rarely comprehend how complex change is and how much time it takes. As American women, we reflect the very culture we seek to change. We need to examine American attitudes toward change and examine ourselves for such cultural hangovers as we investigate how we think we're changed as a result of feminism.

For most Americans the concept of change remains rooted in the material. Any deviation from that acquisitive pattern is met with retaliatory action: gossip, ostracism, even murder. I am not suggesting that feminists share this attitude. We do share, in part, the Good Fairy/Santa Claus syndrome. The fact that it isn't centered around money doesn't lessen the underlying dynamics. Americans have little understanding of cause and effect. We often want results before we've taken appropriate action and few people understand the time and effort it takes for people to change and to develop programs.

The tremendous jolt of feminism is that, at its best, it tries to unite the concept of material change with the concept of emotional/spiritual change. Material change focuses on such issues as child care, abortion and equal pay for equal work. To date, the issue which exemplifies emotional/spiritual change is lesbianism or woman-identification.

Typically, the material issues draw support while the lesbian issue creates outrageous reactions from non-feminists and some feminists alike. Care should be taken, however, to distinguish between the two. While material changes in child care, abortion, etc. would provide breathing space for women, we must recognize that they will not seriously alter the class divisions among women.

These changes, if they came to pass, would not seriously challenge upper-class and middle-class women's control over lower-class women. Just because the control may be indirect--through husbands, fathers, brothers--does not lessen its sting if you happen to be on the receiving end.

Getting stung by other women is also an unfortunate side effect of lesbianism. The inevitability of lesbianism is obvious to anyone who follows the logic of feminism. But, blind to cause and effect, many women in the movement refuse to draw the conclusions of their own theories. It's as though they plant a seed and repudiate the tree.

We reflect American attitudes toward change even within a movement dedicated to change. We also fear those changes which are the greatest and we fear difference: our difference from the rest of society and difference among ourselves on many levels, not just the obvious ones of class, race and lesbianism. Thanks to our Puritan heritage, difference is sin. Change embodies difference. Many of us, internalizing that attitude, turn around and have contempt for women who are where we ourselves were yesterday, forgetting how much oppression we had readily accepted. There is such pressure, internally and externally, to explain ourselves, to explain the changes we are going through, that we are constantly on the defensive and we take offense if a woman can't see it our way.

Change shouldn't mean that you have to justify yourself to anyone, even when they bait you. Nor should it mean you renounce your past and turn into a one-dimensional missionary. Change means you use your past and transform it. Whoever we were, wherever we came from, we did take the risk, and we did change.

The Body Politic

How do feminism and lesbian-feminism change women? Since the physical is the easiest to see but the last to be observed, let's look at how a woman's body is deformed by patriarchy and how feminism corrects that. I especially call your attention to women's bodies because the Women's Movement, due to its largely white, middle-class composition, leans heavily on words at the expense of other forms of communication. As a child raised in a poor, white community I was taught, "Don't listen to what people say, watch what they do." After watching women change as a result of feminism, I'd like to pass on those observations and encourage the reader to become more aware of the non-verbal as one area of that change.

Corsets, bras and the like are superficial devices for molding female flesh to fit male desires. The initial actions of the Women's Movement around these devices appeared superficial and, thanks to a hostile media, were used to make the women appear superficial. However, the shedding of external restrictions doesn't automatically remove learned physical restriction.

Women and men are taught to use space quite differently and we need an in-depth study of this by feminists. Until that study, I offer the following observations.

Lowering a shoulder in the presence of a man, pulling the body in (literally, to take up less space so he can have more), turning the head upward or tilting it to the side, often with persistent eyebrow signals, are motions most non-feminists perform automatically. Such gestures elicit favorable male response. Muscles tighten around a woman's jaw and upper back in the presence of a male. Notice in situations of hostility or fear, any human will tighten. Although the meeting of the sexes is accompanied by protective tension on the part of both parties, men exhibit different strains in keeping with their separate training as the aggressor.

When around men, many women cross and uncross their legs incessantly, modify their voices, open their eyes dramatically, signifying animated interest in the male, and play with their hair. As hair is so important to femininity in America, I take this to be some sort of request for sexual affirmation. Another basic pose of non-feminism is casting the hip slightly forward in male company. Even while being seductive, the non-feminist is careful never to diminish the male's authority. For example, a woman walking with her arm around a man's shoulder would look ridiculous, his waist yes--but only if they are lovers, around his shoulders, never, But a man may put his arm around a woman's shoulders after a brief acquaintance, as he may put his arm around a subordinate male's shoulders...employee, son, etc.

Eye contact is a sure indication of status. Most non-feminists lower the eyes or look to the side, returning a gaze furtively, even more furtively with men. Feminists use more eye level contact than non-feminists and lesbian-feminists sometimes hold their eyes so level in a conversation that it unnerves other non-lesbian women, since this sort of eye contact is considered predatory among heterosexuals.

Voice, much neglected in our visual culture, is as trained for sexist behavior as are other parts of the body. Listen to women and men conversing. A woman usually ends her sentence on a higher note than the rest of the sentence. She clips along at one tone and, at the end, raises her voice almost to the question tone. This rise in tone is a bid for affirmative response. A man does not use this tone-shift when speaking unless asking a direct question. He is taught to end his sentences definitively. It makes him sound as though he knows what he's talking about and a question on your part puts you on the defensive. Feminists hang on to speech patterns, tone and pitch, far longer than to their other oppressed body mannerisms.

Layered on top of these ritualized, learned body movements and patterns are the infinite variety of poses arising from race, class and individual temperament. Feminism alters or destroys postures indicative of second-class status (shuffling) and it is this loss that men bemoan when they claim feminists aren't feminine. Do feminists always stand straight, throw their shoulders back, keep their heads up and look dynamic? Not quite. Bad posture is as American as apple pie. But a feminist's body carries more energy because she drops the oppressed gestures designed to minimize the body's power.

The disappearance of poses resulting from oppression is partly because women in the process of becoming feminists spend more time with other women and those postures look absurd when we're all together. Affecting such postures indicates power relationships and since no woman has the same power over another woman that a man does, the protective gestures are wildly out of place. Few women seem conscious of body changes in this fashion. Even fewer have analyzed this aspect of feminism but everyone feels it. I've seen women tell each other they are acting "too feminine" when what they really were responding to was body gestures.

The first flush of feminism produces a fascinating effect on women. Some undergo a period of heightened tension and awkwardness, almost like adolescence, wherein they unconsciously try to establish a physical identity free of sexist posture. Others lapse into physical apathy. When the woman's identity is established to her own satisfaction, she relaxes and her energy shines through. As you might expect, women studying the martial arts or some athletic pursuit are the most free from oppressed mannerisms and thus radiate an engaging sense of well-being.

As a feminist changes her body, so does the lesbian-feminist. Lesbians use space differently than non-feminists or even most feminists. They project more, use more space and the use is usually forward, i.e., pushing out in front of the body. This is a response to their new physical sense of power. It's a non-verbal demand on the world: Give me room or I'll take it. Because of this, "new" lesbians, lesbians who have come out as a result of the Women's Movement, get into fights with men more quickly than other women. What kindles these incidents is, for the most part, non-verbal. The man assumes a great deal of space (even property right) over a woman who is a stranger to him, intruding into her already narrowed domain, e.g., at a party or on the bus. The two collide because it doesn't occur to him to give way or that he's done something offensive (any woman who is not the private property of one man is the public property of all men). Since she's had a lifetime of giving way and withdrawing spatially, any retreat would be a compromise of her new strength. On the other hand, in situations where the lesbian is not being pushed by men, I have observed less tension in the face and in the back than in most women. She either is less threatened, or more comfortable with men, than the non-feminist and feminist. For some, their relaxation could be that they don't care or are quite unaffected by men.

The woman becoming a lesbian reclaims her sexual power. In discovering her body's power in sexual terms, she eventually experiences multiple orgasms. (Men's reticence in mentioning multiple orgasms is a sign of how that sexual power terrifies them.) A woman with an unusually competent and sensitive man may experience this phenomenon with him. However, if she's with another woman, she has not only her own power to enjoy but also the limitless possibility of another multiple-orgasmic human. Reclaiming sexual power also helps a woman reclaim her aggressiveness. This is one of the reasons even the "loveliest" of lesbians will be called down for "acting like a man." The painful truth is that only men are allowed to have powerful bodies. It's damned if you do and damned if you don't. If a woman keeps oppressed mannerisms, she is called into question by her sisters and if she becomes too strong, she gets censured, again by her sisters.

I have concentrated on the physical because we miss what is right under our noses. Edward T. Hall, in *The Silent Language,* estimates that well over half of human communication is non-verbal, therefore, bodies are tremendously important. If we are to understand how feminism and lesbian-feminism change women then we need to begin with the non-verbal. We must pay as much attention to what we do as to what we say--in fact, more.

The external reflects the internal. As the feminist demands more physical space and reclaims her strength, so too, she seeks increased political space. She is no longer willing to be defined by men, sexually or politically. Our move outward takes aback those accustomed to women "staying in their place," a spatial definition of oppression. We desire and seek participation in the world and we do so without apology. Such a basic change terrifies those unwilling to recognize us as full human beings and irritates those who don't want to share power with us or any other oppressed group. In a world conditioned to viewing us as passive, receptive, supportive and self-effacing, even mild self-assertion seems hot and bold. In an effort to stem the feminist tide, they question our political motives, our establishment credentials, our personal psyches and our physical endowments, desperately looking for any feeble excuse to discredit us. Never have creatures who pretend to measure all reality against Aristotelian paradigms so abandoned logic in their frantic effort to halt change.

While their questions concerning us are hostile and superficial, our own questions concerning ourselves are deeper and more disturbing than those of our detractors. As a woman begins to question woman-oppression, political power is called into question. As she begins to question male supremacy, patriarchy, all of society is called into question. And once she begins to question heterosexuality, the means of male supremacy, she is called into question.

Together as we answer each other and ourselves, we must become aggressive without becoming belligerent. We must take more risks without being foolish. We must harden our bodies and soften our hearts, becoming stronger as we grow more flexible. We cannot repudiate the past nor dare we repeat it. We must challenge our sisters and brothers to change without driving them or belittling them for where they are. We must become more individual as we become one. The more we change the more we realize we must change. There is no end product for us, there is continual process, continual change. I wouldn't want it any other way, would you?

It's All Dixie Cups to Me

Americans have the Dixie-cup mentality--if you don't like someone, then crumple them up and throw them away. Auto graveyards, prisons and mental institutions share one thing in common: all contain society's cast-offs. The truly remarkable aspect of the Dixie-cup mentality is not that Americans throw people and things away but that we assume we can always get another. Cars are replaceable. People are replaceable. All you have to do is look the market over and select the one best suited to your needs.

To complete the cycle of conspicuous abundance and waste we thought we could replace ourselves. And what could be more American? Everyone is out for the best self they can get. Mother called it, "Turning over a new leaf." Religious folk call it, "Rebirth." Madison Avenue sells it as a "New You." Psychology gravely refers to it as an "Identity Crisis." It's all Dixie-cups to me.

Bad as our used car lot attitude toward other people may be, our attitude toward ourselves is even more treacherous. We throw away parts of ourselves we consider unpleasant. Consequently, we suffer head-on collisions with the ghosts of our

But...perpetuated the idea that one can build on identity.

former selves driving down a twisting road that turns in on itself before we can hit the brakes. The need for conscious identity is a manufactured item. The fact that so many people are dismantling and refurbishing themselves turns this phenomena into a bizarre assembly line.

The moment a person dissociates herself from her self, she becomes a spectator to her own life. She becomes schizophrenic. Reality retreats under screening room scrutiny. The self is then once removed from experience. If you aren't your self then, for you, no one else can be a self either. You'll be too busy looking for your self to see other human beings. You'll catch narcissistic paralysis.

There is another self beneath the social self. Social self is self consciousness through comparison. What makes the bedrock self, the root self, so difficult to define is that we owned our self before the moment of comparison.

Can you remember your first moment of self-consciousness? More than likely, that moment involved some kind of comparison. Perhaps you discovered you were black. (Whites didn't discover they were white until 1964.) Or perhaps you found out you were a woman. Maybe someone told you your coat was raggedy and suddenly you knew you were one of the poor. For precious few folk the first moment of self consciousness was not negative. The people who fell into that group discovered they were "better." They discoverd they were men, or rich, or both. Adam knew he was different from the beasts of the land but that self consciousness was not negative. He got to name the beasts, which is power through language. Naming is an expression of status. For those of us who fall into the many oppressed groups, we were named according to our distinguishing feature: nigger, dyke, kike, trash etc. Our early consciousness involved the knowledge that we were "less" or second class.

Through self consciousness we began to look at our selves. By becoming a spectator to our own lives, by comparing, by narrowing our selves, we become removed from our experiences. So removed, we are more in need of external cues to tell us who we are supposed to be. We become vacant and vulnerable, easy targets for manipulation. This vacancy or uncertainty as to place in the social order is one reason advertising is so successful. Consumerism bulldozes a short-cut to identity. It's an echo of school days. You have answers, only now you buy them. The more you buy, the more "right" you are. Objects replace emotions. When the object becomes dated or wears out, you get another one or you lose status. Under these conditons it becomes hard to tell the difference between other humans and objects. Worse, we objectify ourselves. We too become dated as we get older. We aren't as valuable if we aren't lovely, etc.

Self-Service Factories such as Esalen arose in reaction to consumerism. Here one buys the tools to forge a new self. It's psychological consumerism. Phrases from the Self-Service Factories, such as, "get in touch with your feelings," "gut reaction," "I hear you," and others too numerous to mention permeate middle class America. Thanks to television (vicarious identity), those concepts are available to anyone with the stamina to watch "Marcus Welby, M.D." and other media wonders. There is something uniquely American and contradictory in self factories: thousands search uniformly for individuality, for identity. And whose interests does is serve to have vast numbers of the population bellowing the primordial scream in unison?

Such fashionable psychological concepts

seeped into the Women's Movement. Consciousness-raising utilized pop psychology in attacking a
female identity created in oppressive conditions.
But consciousness-raising, the double edged sword
of feminism, also perpetuated the idea that one can
build an identity.

Identity Within The Movement

The Movement was and is correct in stating
that women's collective past bled a river of pain.
The Movement tried to call out what is strong in
women. We tried to find examples from the past.
It's hard for many women to grant that strength to a
living woman in their midst. Woman-hatred again,
dead women are more lovable than living women.
Identifying with other women proved rocky at first
but over time it became easier.

Recognizing that our collective past was as
painful as our individual pasts, the Movement
sought a solution to all that pain and desolation.
Toss away your hateful past and as for a collective
past, dip into the mists of matriarchy, at least life
was better then. With the help of your sisters you
too can build a new and stronger self. When in
doubt pray to the Great Mother in the Skies or Isis
or Sappho.

And here is where we hurt ourselves,
intellectually and organizationally. How are we to
reach others if we deny our past, personal or
collective? We must remember our old, oppressed
selves. We must resolve the pain of our mothers.
We can't blot out that past by ignoring the
thousands of years of male supremacy and nodding
out in the haze of pre-recorded history--matriarchy.
We need to unearth that matriarchal past but it is of
the utmost importance that we don't forget for one

minute what came between us today and matriarchy. We need to understand our past and use it for the future. One of the earmarks of humanness is a conception of the past and a possibility of the future.

Identity, selfhood, cannot be bought, sought or given. A lover, a therapist, the Women's Movement will not make a "new" you. A certain degree of re-evaluation will provide insights into why you did what you did, possibly even helping you see patterns in your behavior. But even that won't tell you who you are. The chilling point is: Why ask? You are you when you "forget" you. Not reject you, not throw your self away like a living Dixie-cup or a worn out Studebaker. Stop looking for a car when you're driving one.

Earlier, I noted that we suffer head-on collisions with the ghosts of our former selves. There's a difference between inspecting your self/past and discarding your self/past. Another way to look at it is to think of your past and the collective past as a boomerang. Throw it away, turn your head and watch out, the boomerang will come back at you. For instance: suppose before you became a feminist you were a dogmatic Lutheran. Now after feminism you are a dogmatic Lesbian. You won't see this repeating pattern because you think you threw the Dixie-cup away. Your friends may see the pattern. Any mention on their part will probably be resented because you thought you'd cut the thread to your oppressed past and your former behavior.

Only by telling who we were and where we came from can another woman know the truth of our journey. Only then can she trust us for we've given her a roadmap.

Feminism, the root self, isn't one magic moment of understanding then life becomes easy.

Feminism begins a process that brings us closer and closer to you/our goal. You'll come home. Home to your root self. Home to the self before social consciousness of self.

The root self, for me, develops from two bases: Emotion and Work. Emotion is the toughest to pin down especially when writing in English. We're told that there is a whole orchestra of emotions. True enough, but I think all emotions spring from two sources: Love and Fear. Fear in its purest stage is a response to physical or mental danger. Fear is reactive. Love is active. Love is the root emotion.

To return to root self we must return to love, a difficult journey in a country that hates women. That is why women-identification, women loving other women, putting women first, putting themselves first is so crucial to our finding our root selves and to us finding the power of our movement.

Love's reality is that it eats away at social structure, at control, so it must be suppressed. Think of the furor over black-white couples. Love threatened a necessary part of racism, that the races remain separate. Or what about cross-class friendships. These are frowned upon, "Stay with your own kind," because in essence, the emotion disrupts oppression.

Love is the enemy of unequal social structure. When people really love they become disobedient. And by love I don't just mean sex because that's a tiny fraction of the love we are capable of. Sex has been used to confine love because it serves male supremacy to limit love to a biological function which keeps us in our place.

After woman-identification, people usually return to some activity they discarded because it was discouraged, Dixie-cupped by parents, teachers, the old gang of psychological thugs. Reinforced by other women and by increasing feelings of strength a woman returns to earlier, lost interests. Re-discovering a happy part of childhood is one more step toward the self before social consciousness of self.

Through my observation, this re-discovery is linked to some form of work. Just as a knowledge of past and future mark us off as human so does the need for fulfilling work, for purpose. A squirrel buries her nuts by instinct. She is born knowing what to do and how to do it. We have to learn. What we learn depends on sex, class and race. Before we suffered consciousness of categorization most of us expressed some preferences about what we liked doing. We liked music or we took clocks apart or whatever. Those pre-school desires, I believe, are close to the root self. An adult going back to that early desire may or may not be able to make a career of it but she'll be getting closer to her self. That renewed strength helps her face a hostile world. It also means she is not going to be content with oppression. She will no longer settle for less. If a woman can make a living from her early work drive she is in an enviable position. She will be especially able to help her sisters since her time won't be divided into earning a wage vs. doing what she wants.

The amazing thing about work is that the more you enjoy your work the harder you work and the less self-conscious you are. You get very close to that root self.

Returning to the root self under male supremacy is a tremendous battle for we must fight the entire Western world as we know it. Under male supremacy love for other humans is labeled irrational, frivolous and so on unless love is within the context of marriage and family where love is one-sided. Once a woman makes the great breakthrough to woman-identification, to discovery of worth, the road becomes smoother although it isn't always safe. We still don't know exactly how a woman becomes woman-identified although we do know the more contact she has with strong, positive women the more likely this will happen.

The Women's Movement, for all our mistakes, is right to hold a mirror up to our faces. By clearly seeing ourselves we can use the jolt of self awareness as an oppressed person to lead us back to our past and simultaneously to our future. By identifying with other women, with ourselves, we gain a definite goal: Freedom. Our self is linked with other selves. The ultimate act of humanness, identifying with others, guides us. Slowly, heightened self-consciousness fades as we connect, understand, love and breathe the lives of our sisters. By identifying with other women some of them begin to identify with us, giving us the love and faith to pursue our work. Within the goal of women's freedom we find our more personal goals.

And one day, in good time, you'll glance in your mirror and discover it's a window. Welcome, Sister, you've come home at last.

The Lady's Not For Burning

What we don't say is as important as what we do say, as individuals and as a political movement. Language determines the structure of our thoughts and, to an extent greater than we realize, determines the structure of feminism. As language provides a clue as to an individual's mental condition so language is a barometer for the sanity of a political movement. First, let me give an example of politics and language far away from feminism. It's easier to see something when it's in somebody else's back yard. Consider Nazi Germany. The Nazis committed unspeakable acts. Repulsive as those acts were they had to find a language to describe them if soldiers were to carry out orders and if the civilian population was to be properly lied to. What the Nazis did was debase the German language. They severely weakened their own tongue to cover up the unspeakable. During the late 1930's and the war few Germans heard the word "death camp." False words were used to cover up the enormity of the murders. Individuals were "relocated" or they disappeared and no word was offered in explanation. The language suffered such ruin that writers of stature did not emerge until the last decade, roughly twenty years after.

People are like volcanoes shooting emotional debris up through the rational crust.

The Nazis understood something crucial to the human intellect: if we can speak of an event we can begin to comprehend it. In order to fool people you must speak euphemisms or nothing at all. In silence comes a linguistic void. Within a void any deed is possible.

In America, heightened during the Nixon years, we observed a parallel attempt to reroute language away from reality to a desired image. A specific example of political watering down of English occurred some ten years ago. The Defense Department ran a project to study the effects of radioactive fallout on the human body. They dubbed this program, Operation Sunshine. That's debasement.

If language is not debased then what is it in its normal state? Essentially language is an equivalency. If I write "grass," "grasshoppers," "Woman running through the grass," you create a picture in your mind that corresponds to grass, grasshoppers and running women you have personally seen or would like to see. However, if I write "freedom," and "feminism," your mental picture blurs a bit. Even though you're a feminist and I'm a feminist my vision of our movement may not be similar to your own. As long as a word equals a material object we run into few problems. Once the word stands for a concept we run into nothing but problems. If there is no word at all but experience nonetheless exists we enter the realm of the frightening, the fanciful, the "impossible."

As Americans we use one of the world's most fluid languages. You can make a noun, an adjective, an adverb, a verb, etc. You can do just about anything with this amazing tool. However, English contains two great weaknesses. One is the tongue is highly judgmental and therefore more subtle than most of its practitioners, particularly Americans, understand. (Save for Southerners, Americans are notoriously indifferent to the beauties of their native language.) The second great weakness which bears heavily on feminists is that English harbors few verbs to properly convey shades of emotion. We can convey via our built in judgments whether an object or deed is good, neutral or bad but when it comes to qualities and intensities of emotion we're barren. For instance, we have one word for love. What else comes close? Affection? Fondness? Desire? Caring? To convey intensity we sputter, "I love you very, very much." Sounds unconvincing and slightly silly. As feminists explore the nature of women's responses to their environment, each other, the self, this verbal gap will create enormous communication difficulties. The deeper you go into emotion the less readily you can convey it. I may grasp for connectives but I will be able to express an entire political program for the transfer of state power before you can tell me the precise sensation of collective euphoria or individual joy.

Keeping the above in mind as well as the Nazi's use of language let's look at feminists and English. We speak of revolution and in America the word revolution is used to sell pantyhose. We do the exact opposite of the Nazis. However, what we do is equally destructive. Feminists *substitute the word for the deed.* Again language no longer corresponds to material reality and soon you weave words to define more words but physically nobody's doing anything. In this kind of betrayal any form of misconduct is possible. If you don't believe that what you are saying is going to be backed up by a deed, do you not begin to doubt your very self? If I don't believe that what you are saying will be made good, how can I bond with you? How can we develop a feminist movement if we're talking rather than acting? Zero trust.

Another paradox of feminist usage of language involves the word "community" and the word "sisterhood." Both imply a togetherness and unity of purpose which presently is in the embryonic stage. The paradox comes from the fact that speech depends on inequality and difference. In order to speak we must be different. If you and I were alike, truly equal and in equilibrium, we need not say a word to one another because you'd already know what I was thinking and feeling. (Many friends and lovers of long standing will tell you they often sustain long silences between them because they know how the other person feels. By contrast when you are "new" to another human, silence, especially for an American, is embarrassing.) As feminists we are currently quite different from one another and we talk a lot. We talk about community revealing how fragile that community is.

Sisterhood dips close to buffoonery. That word was viciously used in 1969 and 1970 to throttle the emerging lesbians who were concretely rather than abstractly loving women. Presently the word sisterhood tolerates a cynical irony of purpose. When preaching sisterhood we often skate into socialism and the idea that we should share our resources. We talk about feminist socialism but we practice laissez-faire economics. The woman who has money keeps it and the woman who doesn't gets nothing from her sisters. Such a blatant contradiction between professed goal and practice builds anything but sisterhood. Again, talk is cheap. Or as my mother taught me, "Watch what people do, don't listen to what they say."

If feminism substitutes the word for the deed and if some words revolve 180 degrees away from their ordinary meaning we can still talk about those things. It's the things we can't talk about that explode like emotional land mines when we create experiences that unwittingly trip them off.

Divide experience into three sections like the spectrum that refracts light passing through it. In the middle of the spectrum blaze the colors of the rainbow which we plainly see with the naked eye. That's where language lives. On either end of the spectrum light exists but humans can't observe it without special equipment. Consider the infra-red end to be the "silence" of the plant and animal world. On the opposite end exists the "silence" of the ultra-violet, the supra-rational or spiritual, for lack of a better word. We humans need listen to both "silences," for experience exists at either end of the spectrum even if we can't describe it.

The Experience Spectrum

Infra-red	Colors	Ultra-Violet
Animal & Plant Life, the Irrational, Silence	Language The Rational	Spiritual Supra-rational Silence

When any human enters into either end of the experience spectrum she is likely to feel terror. If she communicates with a plant she may be frightened not just of the experience but of other humans' responses to it. Humans have no models for such communication and sanity gets threatened. On the cusp of the ultra-violet, literature moves slightly into the rays, music and dance advance the journey even further but there are whole continents about which most of us know nothing and cannot describe although some of us may be able to experience them.

Politically we don't examine what lives on either end of the spectrum. Since language is rational but much of human experience is not we are already pinned down conceptually. There are women moving into the experiental ends, spiritualists, but they cannot yet translate that into political action or language. Hence the latest split between cultural/spiritualists vs. political/realists. Being the good Americans that we are we take up positions and defend them. This gets us nowhere. Perhaps when a spiritual Magellan circumnavigates the globe and comes back to tell the rest of us about the journey then we, too, will believe a new world exists beyond the horizon.

The spiritual-political split covers monsters lurking in the deep. It's what we don't speak about that wrecks us. Unspoken assumptions flourish in subterranean caves motivating behavior but effectively hidden from political view. Following are examples of those monsters, of the silences, the oil slicks and the language double crosses fomenting feminist disorder.

Love. We'll all love one another because we're women. Somehow, like men, we robbed women of their individuality and assumed we'd all be alike. This is emphatically not the case. Because universal love never bloomed some women felt a deep sense of failure. The real hidden assumption was that we couldn't fail.

Another deceptor was egalitarianism. We spoke exhaustingly of equality. Only recently have we been able to discuss the underside of equality which is anti-leadership. Anti-leadership is tied to woman hatred. We still can't trust another woman enough to possibly allow her to represent us in any fashion.

Anti-leadership uncovers national character. Feminists or not, we did grow up in the United States and it did rub off. Americans practice the Great Democratic Contradiction. You elect your leader then you hate him/her. This scapegoating is a self-fulfilling prophecy. Only low life forms flock to politics where they masochistically enjoy the kicks awarded them by their constituents and sadistically relish nailing "enemies" to the wall.

Anti-leadership plays into irresponsibility as well as national character. If you don't acknowledge leaders you aren't honest about your structure. Hidden leaders champion egalitarianism while deviously getting their way. If structure isn't made clear then accountability isn't possible; emotional weight has to be figured into structure.

Small is good. Now this assumption is spoken openly by feminists. Small is supposed to be good because it allows each woman to fully participate in the life of the group. Big is bad. Feminists don't want anything to do with it because women will strangle in frozen heirarchies. What isn't spoken about is the fear of managing large groups. By keeping ourselves small and isolated we are easy to immobilize politically. The reality is this movement is huge, encompassing millions, but the thousands of small groups have not linked with one another. Perhaps what we don't acknowledge is that big means successful in America. Many feminists may die before they admit it but they are terrified of success. Failure, in patriarchal terms, defines woman. Success means you're a ballbuster, acting like a man. Pervasive is the conditioning of women. We must relinquish the luxury of oppression which gives us a rationale for failure and allows us to retreat into moral superiority.

Success uncovers another unspoken monster:

responsibility. If you succeed you make the decisions instead of having them made for you, at you, on you. We all know it's just as easy to make the wrong decision as the right one. You bear the consequences.

The effects of the abovementioned unspoken assumptions are not laudatory. We refuse to elect people out of our midst to represent us. Therefore we must all show up at the same time and in the same place and do the same thing if we are to get anything done. What happens to the woman who can't afford to show up as much as the others? Our perverse egalitarian purity insures a solidly middle class movement because the poor are driven out. Perhaps the only way we can allow ourselves a large organization is to rent the state of Kansas for a weekend and all sit in a circle.

Irony is one thing. Lies are another. Whether a lie or uneasy silence is worse is debatable. In this case the feminist lie involves money. Feminists are all poor. Since I was born poor I'm naturally sensitive to this tampering with the truth. On Halloween, 1975, in San Francisco I asked a group of roughly 700 women to write on a slip of paper their yearly income and to place in a box whatever surplus they might enjoy at the end of that year. I encouraged them to allow plenty of money for clothes, a vacation, entertainment as well as living expenses and then figure their surplus. The group, by the way, was downwardly mobile. If all the work-shirts swayed in unison you'd have gotten seasick. The net income in the room that night was $2,189,875.00. The surplus, which means the money available for one year to fund a project, was $825,976.00. These figures did not take into account inheritance, stocks, bonds or property so the figure would be well over one million dollars if those were figured in on a percentage basis. If feminists put their money where their movement is we'd WIN.

Perhaps one of the reasons we lie about money involves conflict. Unspoken is the idea that conflict is evil. If we lie about money, if we hide our power structures, if wo diffuse responsibility, it's much harder to get into a good fight over differences. That difference exists is indisputable. Conflict is smothered like leadership, financial responsibility and success. Could it be we're afraid we're not strong enough to weather the storm? Rather than be uncomfortable for an hour, or wax hot in a feud, we'll wait five months for it to come back at us and take our head off when we least expect it. Conflict has to come out somewhere in some way. Better to get it out honestly and solve the problem rather than intensify it by denial.

This avoidance allows only one mechanism for disagreement and that is separatism. Separatism from men is one thing. Separatism from each other is quite another. If feminists refuse to risk a fight to solve our "minority" problems, are we any better than the United States government which refuses to solve them, too?

Hidden though they may be these unspoken assumptions can be clarified when brought to the light of language. Grammar alone demands that we order chaotic experience. The idea of the rational, the mainspring of all linguistic structure, is also at the heart of feminism. Like all other revolutions we operate on the idea that people are rational. Or a modified version of that is: other people may be irrational but feminists are rational. We can reconstruct society and it's going to work. Humans possess all the years since 1789 to prove we do not rationally reconstruct our societies. We never quite take this into account. The irrational rests on the horizon of language: we aren't pushing ourselves to cross that horizon. The dim shadow of the guillotine still casts itself over our future.

People are like volcanoes shooting emotional debris up through the rational crust. Early in the movement we dimly recognized that and developed consciousness raising but that only took us so far. Then feminist therapy took over. Spiritualists may take us one step further.

Sports might be a way to deal with the irrational and the suprarational. Mind and body are not separate. We've done little work in this area because it isn't considered intellectual (verbal) and therefore suffers low status. We've betrayed ourselves by not encouraging feminist coaches and athletes to learn more and teach us what they know. The idea of sports contributing to a revelation or a new perception of ourselves no doubt sounds incredible to some of you. Your incredulity is proof enough of the disdain with which Puritan America holds the human body.

Art traditionally flirts with the irrational and the suprarational. Feminists gradually are allowing artists to challenge them rather than play to their base theatrical instincts. Perhaps the way for artists is easier than the way for athletes because prior models exist, i.e., Mao's talk at the Yenan conference.

So far the monsters swimming up from the depths might make us uncomfortable but none of them shakes the foundations of our belief system. Here I come to the most terrifying assumption in the movement. Feminists hold at their core the very same thing which is at the core of patriarchy and that is *principle*. Principle before people. You adopt a system of thought (Jesus, Marx, Freud, Feminism), you defend it and you cut people off who do not agree with you. While currently not as vile as patriarchs about principle we act on it all the same. Principle is first. People are second. Flesh and blood are not as worthy a commitment as the idea and the ideal. We pledge ourselves to the ideal. I am now convinced that this pledge is the root of the inhuman. Underneath principle lies the fear of difference. Principle demands that we think alike, act alike and possibly even look alike. The iron mask of conformity mocks us beneath our chatter of multiplicity. Think of the controversy over body hair. Think what would happen if I gave a speech to a feminist audience while wearing a skirt? We still have trouble with difference. If we didn't have trouble with difference we'd have solved classism, racism and sex preference within our own movement. And we'd have made some progress on the less obvious differences: regional background, body type, age, etc. Are we so abysmally weak we can not tolerate difference much less enjoy it?

The solution of patriarchy to difference was to mutilate the flesh to save the soul. (Mind-body split again.) You burn the witch but her immortal soul flies up to heaven, purified.

In our movement do we not mistrust the flesh as deeply as the patriarch? We mistrust the bond, a bloodknot, tied with another human being. Surely love of country comes before love of wife for a patriarchal man. What's our parallel? If feminists didn't have this mistrust would lesbianism have been the explosive issue it turned out to be? Lesbianism is the symbol for the flesh in the feminist movement. It represents the bond one woman makes to another. Ideologues would rather we stick to the political ramifications of lesbianism and love all women. That's how seductive the idea of principle is to all of us. Principle cannot allow for pleasure because if people are happy you can no longer control them. Pleasure need be organized and doled out in a way that serves the appropriate political interest.

This lust after principle does something else. It disassociates a person from her identity. Principle comes between you and you. You want to do something but you have a duty which conflicts with that desire. It is this disassociation from yourself that can make you dangerous. You can be more easily manipulated because you aren't whole. You look for pieces to fill up the emptiness: drugs, drink, religion, sex, even revolutionary politics. If you are separated from yourself how can you know who you are? How can you know who another woman is and allow her her identity, individuality, difference? You'll deny her her lesbianism, her Blackness, her class roots. You'll deny her whatever it is that makes you vaguely aware of your own emptiness. The further away you get from yourself the closer you approach the inhuman. How long before one of us kills another because she is not a true revolutionary feminist? Principle before people.

Below the disassociation of self lurks one more assumption: Individual needs and societal wants are in conflict. In order for society to function, its selfish members must be taught sacrifice. All of patriarchal culture is based on that conflict: individual vs. society. Society and the individual may not be in conflict at all. Humans do not have to be reared on a sacrifice mentality. As long as patriarchs run the world that will be the model. As long as we do not speak the unspoken that will be our unacknowledged model as well.

Are we so lacking in imagination that we can't harmonize society and the individual within it? Are we going to commit a re-run revolution? Will we, fearing the flesh and fearing difference, begin to burn our witches? This lady's not for burning.

I believe we can honor life in the living of it. I believe we can gather the light if we take the chance and thrust our hands in the fire. I believe we can restructure patriarchy into something, not perfect, but far more gentle. How? I leave you with that, with no easy answers, no magic solution. I'm doing my part. You do yours. And so I leave you as we both began, in profoundest silence.

Conclusion

It is impossible for small feminist units by themselves to effect the salvation of society or even to survive in the teeth of patriarchy. This parallels the isolated communist islands that drowned in a 19th Century sea of capitalism, (i.e., the Oneida Community). In order to defeat patriarchy we must build large scale organizations that focus our energies and keep our political enemies off balance. Without this shield we can be picked off one by one. A rape crisis center can be shut down in Hartford, Connecticut and the rape crisis center in New York City does nothing to help, either because women there don't know what's happening to the north of them or because they feel powerless to assist. However, a strong national organization of rape crisis centers could back up Hartford and fight it out with the "authorities" seeking to close it down. Think what would happen if the national rape crisis centers linked up with the national health care centers, and the women's centers, etc., etc. Then we just might have the basis for a real struggle against Tweedledee and Tweedledum: the captains of industry and the U.S. government.

Everything which later became a party was at first a sect. Remember you and I are sowing seeds.

. . .you and I are sowing seeds. One of them will surely sprout.

One of them will surely sprout.

I would like to leave you with three seeds I think will help us gradually develop a strong power base. These programs are stepping stones. They are necessary for our political victory but not sufficient.

Two of the programs, feminist assemblies and sports leagues, are really sketches. You will need to do the actual painting. The third program, a feminist organizer's school, is more complete.

Feminist Assemblies

Our movement is ten years old. Within those ten years we have not addressed ourselves to the problem of representing ourselves to one another, developing political priorities and acting on those priorities. Our feminist media struggles along according to whoever has the energy to run a newspaper. Our political projects are small, isolated, often unreliable or amateurish. Such disarray does not inspire political confidence in people who might be sympathetic to feminism.

For the last two hundred years we have not been represented fairly in the House of Representatives, the Senate, the Supreme Court, or the Executive Branch of the U.S. government. Washington, D.C. is the only city in the world where sound travels faster than light but they certainly don't want to hear what feminists have to say. So we must speak to one another.

Feminists in each state must create a Feminist Assembly so we can communicate to each other in a responsible fashion. The state system has drawbacks but we will need to start at a state level because of the manner in which states' rights is currently being used to oppress women and gay people.

The first Assembly should be in session for two weeks. Representatives should be paid. No more Lady Bountiful. Given that we can't afford to pay anyone for a year's work and given that we can't afford to rent facilities for a year we will need to start with two weeks preferably in the summer because this gives the femInist with a straight job the opportunity to use her vacation time to become a representative if she is elected.

Each feminist group from all over the state should elect one representative. After the first session the representatives will have hammered out a more adequate system of representation. Your first assembly will strongly resemble the Constitutional Convention of the United States held at the end of the Eighteenth Century. You will need to solve the same problems. Do you elect representatives on the basis of the size of the group or do you elect one woman from each feminist group? Some states may pick one solution over the other, some may arrive at the same solution as the Convention; a House based on population and a Senate based on a set number for each group. It's vital for each state to find its own way.

The duties of the Feminist Assembly should be communicating the will of the feminist community, solving the problems of the various communities, ordering statewide political priorities both in terms of patriarchal politics (i.e., elections, strikes, equal opportunity employment, consumer revenge, etc.) and the priorities of feminist politics (i.e., creating separate spaces for women to go to in order to revive and be reborn, feeding our own people, developing programs to help women who aren't feminists and dispelling the patriarchal slander aimed at us). None of this is easy.

Unanimous decisions will be extremely rare but once a decision is reached it is the duty of the representatives and the community she represents to carry out the decisions of the Assembly.

The Assembly serves other functions. We create a counter-government to the existing government without directly *physically* challenging that government. That challenge may indeed come decades later but for now it is important to collect ourselves without wild claims that we represent the people and not the United States Senate. We develop skills that will enable some of us to get elected to the patriarchal government and work from the inside. We develop skills at solving our own problems. We learn to respect one another through contact, disagreement, compromise and hard work. We show one another that we can do what we say. One successful project is worth a thousand brilliant paper ones.

Each year, hopefully, the Assembly can meet for a longer period of time. Each year, hopefully, the local communities will make a deeper commitment to financially supporting the assembly. The form of financing will be chosen by the community but I repeat, it is essential that women get paid for their labor. The Catholic Church has survived for 1,976 years through tithing. Tiny towns in Latin America with poor populations have beautiful churches. Surely, we can tithe ourselves for our state assembly and meet the needs of our people better than the Catholic Church meets the needs of its poor parishoners.

The question of what is a feminist group I also leave up to individual groups and the states. To me, a feminist group is any group pledged to advancing the cause of women, most especially gaining political power. A health care center may not be directly involved in gaining political power but it does meet the needs of women and challenge the entrenched, anti-woman medical profession so I consider it a feminist group. It's far more important for you all to answer these questions with one another than for me to do so even if I had all the magic answers. And that's the whole point of the Assembly--to put women together in the same room to work out our mutual problems and to develop a common political program.

From state assemblies, in time, we move to regional assemblies and finally a national assembly. But we have to start somewhere and I suggest your own back yard.

Physical Power

Women do not control the most basic geography of all, our own bodies. Submission is a product of physical weakness. Patriarchs like their women weak, soft, etc. Only recently have Americans begun to tolerate the concept of the woman athlete. As children our identity is tied into physical prowess. Little girls, discouraged from sports, grow into women incapable of defending themselves not because they can't but because they don't know how and because they perceive themselves as weak. A strong person is much less likely to be anyone's victim, personally or politically.

Feminists must create sports programs in their area to serve the needs of all women. Special emphasis should be placed on little girls. The YWCA can be particularly helpful here. It isn't necessary to get into ideological arguments about feminism and the purpose of the YWCA. All you need to do is use the facilities. My experience with the YWCA has been that YWCA women are genuinely concerned about the status of women and dedicated to health.

If there is a feminist coach or competitor (female or male) in your area ask her if she would be willing to set up and run, if at all possible, a program for your area. Keep in mind that women in physical education are terrified of public lesbianism because of the manner in which their profession has been downgraded by our society.

Explore the various sport societies, i.e. Turners for gymnastics, to see if additional programs for women can be developed through them.

Magazines like *Sportswoman* and *Womensports* may be setting up athletic scholarships through their own foundations. With proper negotiating those publications may be willing to help you coordinate a sports program. For instance if squash is important to you they could tell you where the various squash clubs exist, what is their policy on women (until recently women were not allowed membership in squash clubs), who are the best athletes, what are the resources in the field and who else might be willing to help you in this project.

Individual athletes themselves are constantly hit upon for this cause or that cause. Some, such as B.J. King, work for the advancement of women in professional sport. We can only hope that many more of these champions will put themselves on the line to help. Again, don't clobber these women with ideological arguments. They've spent their lives working to achieve perfection in their field. Chances are good they haven't been studying feminist philosophy but they do understand how women are cheated in sports and they especially understand how other countries are serious about women athletes while the U.S.A. lags far behind. Whether in sports or any area of human endeavor approach people from their area of interest, not yours.

The hardest areas to develop will be, as in everything else, poverty areas. It is here more than in Scarsdale where girls and women need assistance, medical care and encouragement. You might be able to tie in with a local health care clinic for medical attention.

In the past *Ms.* Magazine sponsored the *Ms.* mile in Madison Square Garden. The track event proved a huge success. It isn't unreasonable to think that magazines such as *Viva* and *Playgirl* might be willing to sponsor a particular event once a year, such as a gymnastics meet. The magazines get publicity and the young athletes have a much needed opportunity to receive media attention, gain competitive experience and meet each other. A five-year-old girl seeing a fourteen-year-old young woman working the uneven bars will be forever impressed. She'll want a strong body, too.

Many large city newspapers are adding women reporters to their sports writing staffs thanks to the phenomenal interest in women's sports evidenced by their readers. When you want coverage call the reporter. Chances are she will cover your program.

Our Roman foremothers preceded us into the sports arena. "Sens mena, sens corpora," they said--a sound mind in a sound body. As feminists we need it now more than ever.

Feminist Organizers' School

The following program is a focused curriculum for one year. The purpose of this school is to train women, sharpen their existing skills and provide ideological perspective so they can return to their communities to carry out feminist projects. These skills bear on a common political goal which is the transfer or at the least the sharing of state power with/from those men who now hold it to those of us who do not. This school makes no claims for concocting instant utopia. Our need is to begin the social/political economic restructuring we so desperately need and to provide people with the tools to accomplish that end. Another way to look at the school is that it concentrates on undermining the oppressor's power base while expanding and consolidating our own.

The school should consist of 100 students. If it grows over the years, naturally, more courses, faculty, students will be added. Four administrators (overburdened, admittedly) can perform fund-raising, public relations and paying the bills. Between seven and ten women will constitute the faculty. Administration and faculty are paid no less than the minimum wage and hopefully they will be paid equivalent to what a state university would pay an associate professor. Women's labor must be *valued.*

If administration and faculty can be considered stable elements, remaining over the years, participating in decisions over curriculum, hiring, etc. then students must also have a voice in these proceedings even though they are a transient population. The obvious structure of a student legislature should not be overlooked as well as seven students being elected to sit on the governing board of the school. Ten years in the movement have taught me that as people filter through a project each group, like a generation, must learn certain things. Think of each woman's confrontation with lesbianism as a parallel. No matter how politically advanced the original lesbian-feminists become, each "new" woman coming out or choosing heterosexuality must face lesbianism as a personal/political issue. That face off occurs over a period of years and exhibits stages of growth, recognition, resolution. So it is with all political issues. Each new political "generation" will water down the long range goals of the school if their particular stage of growth overshadows the priorities of the school. It's a little like a new but good tennis player wanting to rush the net and put them all away. It takes years to master the subtlety of the game. Staying at the baseline and lobbing, while not as exciting, might be the way to win. The essence of successful politics is in developing priorities and sticking to them with a degree of flexibility. Therefore, while students must be part of the decision making process their number on the governing board must remain a minority. Being a minority will also help teach the delegates the techniques of coalition, i.e. with the faculty. The classical strategy of secession is open to any group that violently disagrees with a policy. They can go form their own school. The necessity is that the goals remain intact for this institute.

Class time will be highly structured. That time must focus on facts, process, how to do things. If one learns to repair an automobile one does not sit around the lame vehicle and chant, "Om-m-m." So it is with political education. We must learn how an economic crankshaft is connected to a feminist engine block.

The curriculum is divided into a strategic model and a tactical model:

The Strategic Model

Each woman must take one course specializing in one of the following nations. Emphasis will be on economic structures, the role of women and how a power transfer was successfully organized:

Russia	1870-1976
China	1921-1976
Germany	1870-1945

Each woman is required to take all of the following:

⊙ Feminist history in the U.S. and Canada with equal emphasis on patriarchal domestic policies.

⊙ Conflict resolution

⊙ Leadership as a function of all political structures, emphasis on feminist discoveries

⊙ The nature of the multi-national corporation

Electives are as follows:

⊙ Relation of body to mind, theory as well as body work

⊙ The American character, a psychological study

⊙ Art as a weapon and a prophecy

⊙ Violence and non-violence in relation to political effectiveness

The Tactical Model

Before attending the school each student must prepare a great deal of research. This will be under written supervision of an instructor. The student's research model will be her own city, town or rural community. This will reinforce a little more roots and a little less grass in our grass roots movement.

The following three areas will be researched:

I.   Political power in the comminity

II. Food, clothing, shelter, the quality of life

III. Field work--applying theory to reality and vice versa

I. Political Power in the Community

Often small towns are more corrupt than big cities since a small number of people hold office and usually control the economic life of the town at the same time. Also, big city government, since face to face contact is weakened, is easier to attack. Bucking the power structure in a small town involves a higher risk since personal relationships are often upset.

The student begins by making a chart of power in her community. She should be able to tell, as well as anyone who looks at her chart, just where the power resides. For instance, by consulting her model, she will be able to tell if it's possible to get money out of the existing structure for a particular project.

To give you a better idea, attached are two power charts. One for the city of Boston and another for the town of Provincetown, Massachusetts.

II. Food, clothing, shelter

A. Food
1. Are there food co-ops in your area? How do they work?
2. Is it possible to use food co-ops as an organizing tool?
3. Do farmers in your area grow cash crops or crops for local consumption? Are the farms individually owned or owned by conglomerates? Is there such a thing as a dairy cooperative in your area?
B. Shelter
1. In a low income project is rent withholding possible to win better services?
2. If you live in a city how do you organize

Boston

Boxes are separate political bodies. The lines show how they are connected.

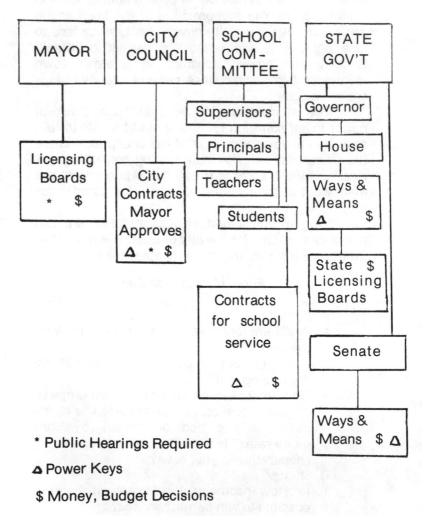

| MAYOR | CITY COUNCIL | SCHOOL COM-MITTEE | STATE GOV'T |

Supervisors

Governor

Licensing Boards * $

City Contracts Mayor Approves Δ * $

Principals

House

Teachers

Ways & Means Δ $

Students

State $ Licensing Boards

Contracts for school service Δ $

Senate

Ways & Means $ Δ

* Public Hearings Required

Δ Power Keys

$ Money, Budget Decisions

Provincetown, Massachusetts

Direct Power, 10 Men

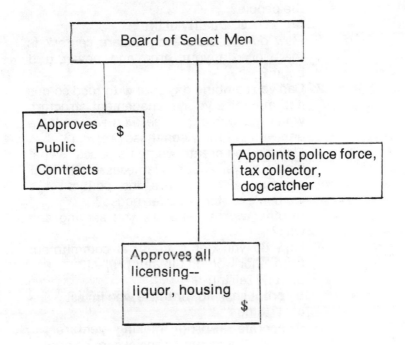

Note public hearings are not required nor encouraged.

$ Money, budget decisions

block by block? Who are the existing leaders on the blocks? (A leader needs no title, she can run the grocery store on the corner.)

3. How did the local leaders win the trust of the people?

C. Quality of life

1. How do you start a child care center? Is there one in your area and how did it begin?

2. Can you combine day care with food co-ops and minimize your management structure while maximizing those women available and willing to work on these projects?

3. How do you create women's space? What kind of physical space is necessary in your community? What are the politics of a women's center or coffee house?
In other words, who are you serving and why?

4. How do you get a financial commitment from other women for your project?
   a. fund raising
   b. profit sharing for those who invest
   c. tithing
   d. operate a profit making venture which helps fund a social service project

5. If there are feminist projects in your community, how are decisons made? Report how these projects actually work, not how you or the participants think they should work.

III. Field Work

After the tactical model is completed and the instructor's written observations assimilated, the student attending the school will take a class specifically designed to examine her own material and the material of other women. Together with other students each woman will develop a time-table for organizing a specific political goal which she chooses, i.e. the feminist assembly. Through the class she will see where her area parallels other women's and where it is different.

It will become apparent to the student that the tactical model relates to the strategic model. She will be stimulated by understanding, for instance, that what happened in China in 1933 might be directly related to her project.

As the student's work continues she will be called in for a conference with each of her instructors before she leaves the school. They will inform her of her progress, her weak points and her strong points. Once the student leaves the school she may return as she finds necessary. She may also recommend women from her community who she feels should attend the school. The school, with her approval, may assist her over the years in finding current students who will, when leaving, go work with her. In this way, over the years, the original student does not remain the primary "trouble-maker" in her area nor can she dominate the feminist community. By this process of expansion the leadership base is broadened and continually replenished by other women. As time passes these new women, coming into the community, will be younger and younger than our original student. In this way we transmit knowledge to our own generations. If the chain of knowledge is broken, as it was in 1920, it will take decades to pick up the struggle where it was cut off. We cannot afford such a rupture.

If the school takes root I would like to see it add summer sessions and night courses to enable people to participate who can't take one year off.

Students will have to pay to attend this school. The fee depends on the facilities. If the school must provide dorms and food, obviously the fee will be higher than if students find their own living quarters. As small colleges close it is not unreasonable to hope we can buy one. In the last century, women's colleges, revolutionary at that time, were started by determined women. By perserverance they raised the money, often from wealthy women who came, in time, to believe in their cause. If they could do it one hundred years ago we can do it today. The larger our endowment, the more scholarships we can offer. Do it.

You may ask about the rigorous program outlined. It is my experience that people usually do not push themselves hard enough, especially intellectually. The present state of feminism is living proof that people refuse to do their "homework." The requirements are structured to encourage the student to learn and to deliver that knowledge to others, her community. A woman should come to this school with the idea in mind that for one year's time she is going to work harder than she has ever worked in her life. That one year will serve her for all the rest of the years of her life. It will be worth all the pressure, all the work, and all the friends she'll make while attending.

Aside from the obvious aforementioned political purpose of this school there is another: to teach women to think in centuries not days. This struggle will and must go through many phases, many years. Think of it as reincarnations, if you will.

Roger, Wilco, Over and Out

Since *A Plain Brown Rapper* looks back over the last ten years and presents political projects for our next ten years, what about my own personal future?

I'll write fiction until the day I breathe my last. Given that only the good die young I'll be writing fiction for some time to come.

In non-fiction terms I'd like to write a book on the multinational corporation and what it means to feminists. To give you a sneak preview, a movement without a solid economic base is like a car without an engine. To date most feminists have either ignored economics or borrowed slavishly from the Left. Marxism is an event in intellectual and political history but if you stop there don't be surprised if the world passes you by. We need to examine not just economic theory but the way things actually work. Only by understanding physical reality can you hope to change it.

Change is the mainspring of feminism and my mainspring as well. The excitement of this movement has not dimmed for me in all these years. I get angry and exhausted but never bored. Somedays I dream I'll ride the Staten Island ferry and build an international feminist organization as I glide beneath the lamp of liberty and behold those ponderous stone breasts. Other days I just know she'd drop her torch on me for spite. But every day I understand a little more clearly that I am only one of millions. If you read all the way through this book you're in this movement, too, I figure, another one among the millions. You by now have a pretty good idea of what direction I'm heading in and how I think. You might agree with much of what I write and then again you might be furious. Whichever way you lean if you get nothing else from this book or me, get this: you are every bit as responsible for this movement as I am. If you don't like the programs I outlined don't waste time bitching about how stupid I am. You come up with a better program. And if you like the programs don't waste time praising me (well, you can take a few minutes to cheer), improve the design. We can't wait for a feminist Messiah, we have to do it all by ourselves. In other words, you can no longer look for the answer. You must be the answer.

PERMISSIONS

I wish to thank the following publications in which my essays first appeared: *Rat, Come Out!, The Ladder, off our backs, Women: a journal of liberation, The Furies,* and *Quest: a feminist quarterly.*

Violence was the text of a speech given at the first Congress to Unite Women in the fall of 1969.

Coitus Interruptus was first published in *Rat,* February, 1970 and was reprinted in *The Ladder,* April-May, 1971.

Yale Break was first published in *Rat,* February, 1970.

Something About "Walk a Mile in My Shoes" was first published in *Rat,* February, 1970.

Say It Isn't So was first published in *Rat,* March, 1970 and was reprinted in *The Ladder,* June-July, 1970.

August 26, 1970, N.Y.C. was published in *Come Out!,* Sept-Oct., 1970.

Hanoi to Hoboken: a round trip ticket was first published in *off our backs,* March, 1971.

Living With Other Women was first published in *Women: a journal of liberation,* June, 1971.

Take a Lesbian to Lunch was first published in *The Ladder,* April-May, 1972.

The Last Straw was first published in *Motive: the lesbian-feminist issue,* winter, 1972.

The Shape of Things to Come was first published in *Women: a journal of liberation,* January, 1972.

Roxanne Dunbar was first published in *The Furies,* January 1972.

Gossip was first published in *The Furies,* January, 1972.

Leadership vs. Stardom was first published in *The Furies,* February, 1972.

The Last Picture Show was first published in *The Furies,* March-April, 1972.

A Manifesto for the Feminist Artist was first published in *The Furies,* June-July, 1972

Love Song for Feminists from Flamingo Park was first published in *off our backs,* September, 1972.

I Am A Woman was first published in *off our backs,* October, 1972.

The Good Fairy was first published in *Quest: a feminist quarterly,* Summer, 1974.

It's All Dixie Cups to Me was first published in *Quest: a feminist quarterly,* Winter, 1975.